Twayne's United States Authors Series

EDITOR OF THIS VOLUME

Warren French

Indiana University

Lillian Hellman

TUSAS 338

LILLIAN HELLMAN

By KATHERINE LEDERER

Southwest Missouri State University

TWAYNE PUBLISHERS

A DIVISION OF G. K. HALL & CO., BOSTON

Printed on permanent/durable acid-free paper and bound
in the United States of America

First Printing

Frontispiece photograph of Lillian
Hellman by Joyce Dopkeen/The
New York Times.

Library of Congress Cataloging in Publication Data

Lederer, Katherine.
Lillian Hellman.

(Twayne's United States authors series; TUSAS 338)
Bibliography: p. 144–51
Includes index.
1. Hellman, Lillian, 1905–   —Criticism and interpretation.
PS3515.E343Z76   812'.5'2   79-12104
ISBN 0-8057-7275-8

For
Nina Campbell Lipscomb, Katherine Gay,
Margaret Lipscomb, Susan Lederer, and
Geoffrey Lederer

Contents

About the Author

Katherine Lederer was born in Trinity, in East Texas in 1932. She received her B.A. from Sam Houston State University, her M.A. and Ph.D. from the University of Arkansas. She is a professor of English at Southwest Missouri State University, Springfield, where she teaches American drama, American novel, and science fiction.

She has served on the Springfield Little Theatre Board of Directors, and she is currently vice-president and a member of the Board of Directors of The Sound of Jazz, Inc., Springfield's jazz society.

Preface

Lillian Hellman is the author of eight original plays, beginning with *The Children's Hour* in 1934. Two of these plays won the Drama Critics' Circle award. In addition, she has written three best-selling memoirs, one of which won the National Book Award. Yet there are few critical studies of her work, and the existing criticism deals with Hellman as a writer of "well-made melodramas."

While presenting the standard criticism of Hellman's work, I have also attempted in this book to demonstrate that the key to judging Hellman is to examine a way of "seeing" rather than to apply traditional generic nomenclature.

I have not attempted to rank her in relation to her contemporaries. The theme of the discussion is that her best plays are ironic and novelistic, that her work differs sharply from that of her fellow American playwrights and must be viewed accordingly. For those who do not accept this argument, the traditional views are amply covered. It is my belief, however, that a reexamination of Hellman's work and of the use of the techniques of irony in that work will support the validity of my presentation.

Since judgments of Hellman's private actions and public statements have often affected critical judgments of her work, I have included a brief biography, but space limitations of the format of this series have prevented inclusion of analyses of her adaptations of others' theatrical works or of her own film scripts and film adaptations of her plays.

Newspapers cited in the text without the name of the city are from New York. The following abbreviations are used in text citations of newspapers and magazines: *DN* (New York *Daily News*), *HT* (New York *Herald Tribune*), *JA* (New York *Journal-American*), *LHJ* (*Ladies' Home Journal*), *NR* (*New Republic*), *NY* (*New Yorker*), *NYRB* (*New York Review of Books*), *NYT* (*New York Times*), *NYTBR* (*New York Times Book Review*), *SR* (*Saturday Review*), *WTS* (New York *World-Telegram and Sun*). *WW* is used for *Writers at Work*.

All quotations from Lillian Hellman's plays are taken from *The Collected Plays* (Boston, 1972); quotations from other works by Miss Hellman are identified by *P* (*Pentimento*), *ST* (*Scoundrel Time*), and *UW* (*An Unfinished Woman*).

KATHERINE LEDERER

Springfield, Missouri

Acknowledgments

I thank Warren G. French, Sylvia E. Bowman, Alberta M. Hines, Alice D. Phalen, Carol S. Cerino, Norma Fryatt, Bud Morton, Lenore Tomlinson, Ben D. Kimpel, Claude W. Faulkner, George Gleason, William Bedford, Robert Henigan, Billie Hurst, Judy Reynolds, and the SMSU Faculty Research and Leave Committees.

The author gratefully acknowledges permission to quote from the following: *The Children's Hour*: Copyright 1934 by Lillian Hellman; copyright renewed © 1961 by Lillian Hellman. By permission of Harold Matson Company, Inc.

Days to Come: Copyright 1936 by Lillian Hellman; copyright renewed © 1964 by Lillian Hellman. By permission of Harold Matson Company, Inc.

The Little Foxes: Copyright 1939 by Lillian Hellman; copyright renewed © 1966 by Lillian Hellman. By permission of Harold Matson Company, Inc.

Watch on the Rhine: Copyright 1941 by Lillian Hellman; copyright renewed © 1968 by Lillian Hellman. By permission of Harold Matson Company, Inc.

The Searching Wind: Copyright 1944 by Lillian Hellman; copyright renewed © 1971 by Lillian Hellman. By permission of Harold Matson Company, Inc.

Another Part of the Forest: Copyright 1946 by Lillian Hellman as an unpublished work. Copyright 1947 by Lillian Hellman. By permission of Harold Matson Company, Inc.

Toys in the Attic: Copyright 1959 by Lillian Hellman. By permission of Harold Matson Company, Inc.

The Autumn Garden: Copyright 1951 by Lillian Hellman. By permission of Little, Brown and Co.

An Unfinished Woman: Copyright © 1965, 1966, 1969 by Lillian Hellman. By permission of Little, Brown and Co.

Pentimento: Copyright © 1973 by Lillian Hellman. By permission of Little, Brown and Co.

Scoundrel Time: Copyright © 1976 by Lillian Hellman. By permission of Little, Brown and Co.

Chronology

1906*	June 20, Lillian Florence Hellman born in New Orleans, Louisiana to Max and Julia (Newhouse) Hellman.
1911	Family moves to New York, N.Y.
1924– 1925	Graduates from Wadleigh High School in New York; attends New York University; works for Boni and Liveright Publishing House; writes reviews for New York *Herald Tribune*; works as play reader.
1925	December 31, marries Arthur Kober.
1925– 1930	Lives in Paris, then Hollywood, working as script reader.
1930	Meets Dashiell Hammett. Returns to New York.
1932	Divorces Kober.
1934	*The Children's Hour*.
1935	*The Dark Angel* (film).
1936	*Days to Come; These Three* (film adaptation of *The Children's Hour*).
1937	*Dead End* (film).
1939	*The Little Foxes*.
1941	*Watch on the Rhine*; Hellman wins Drama Critics' Circle award; *The Little Foxes* (film).
1943	*Watch on the Rhine* (film); *The North Star* (film).
1944	*The Searching Wind*.
1946	*The Searching Wind* (film); *Another Part of the Forest*.
1948	Hellman blacklisted in movie industry; *Another Part of the Forest* (film).
1949	*Montserrat* (adaptation of Emmanuel Roblès' play); *Regina* (Marc Blitzstein adaptation of *The Little Foxes* as an opera).
1951	*The Autumn Garden*.
1952	Revival of *The Children's Hour*; Hellman testifies before House Un-American Activities Committee (HUAC).
1955	*The Lark* (adaptation of Jean Anouilh's *L'Alouette*).
1956	*Candide* (libretto by Hellman, music by Leonard Bernstein, lyrics by Richard Wilbur).

1960	*Toys in the Attic*; wins Drama Critics' Circle award.
1961	January, Dashiell Hammett dies.
1963	*My Mother, My Father and Me* (adaptation of Burt Blechman novel *How Much?*).
1967	June, Dorothy Parker dies; Hellman named executor of will; *The Little Foxes* (all-star revival at Lincoln Center).
1969	*An Unfinished Woman* (memoir, wins the National Book Award).
1972	*Collected Plays*.
1973	*Pentimento* (memoir).
1976	*Scoundrel Time* (Hellman's memories of McCarthy period).

*Hellman's father, like many of his generation with European backgrounds, spoke of his daughter as being six, for instance, on her fifth birthday. Hence, for years her birthdate has been incorrectly given as 1905.

CHAPTER 1

Life and Times

The reader knows the writer better than he knows himself; but the writer's physical presence is light from a star that has moved on—John Updike

I *Early Success on Broadway and in Hollywood*

LILLIAN Hellman has been a considerable figure in the American theater for forty years. In that time critics have made judgments of her work based on assumptions about her Southern background and her political commitments, assumptions which a study of the biographical data proves unwarranted. For example, as recently as 1963, an interviewer asked her how she felt when she "came North" with her first play, *The Children's Hour*. Miss Hellman reminded him that she had come North twenty-four years before that play and had grown up in New York City.

Although she spent enough time in the South during those years to be knowledgeable about its manners, traditions, and customs, it would be more accurate to describe her background as urban-Jewish. Miss Hellman grew up not on a plantation, but in an apartment on 95th Street, between Riverside Drive and West End Avenue. But she *was* born in the South, in New Orleans, on June 20, 1906. Her grandfather, Bernard Hellman, had emigrated in 1848 to New Orleans, which even then had a strong Jewish community. He married Babette Kochland, and their son, Max, married Julia Newhouse of Demopolis, Alabama. Until the publication of *An Unfinished Woman*, Hellman had said little about her family. She described her father as "kind of bright and funny—gay, full of life and interested in everything," her mother as "a gentle, very pleasant woman, nice-mannered—an innocent woman" (*Post*, Mar. 6, 1960). Once, when an interviewer asked her about real-life prototypes for the Hubbards of *The Little Foxes*, Miss Hellman said, "Lots of people thought it was my mother's family" (*WW*, p. 121). *An Unfinished Woman* makes it clear that her mother's family did

1

indeed serve as models for the Hubbards. Her experiences with her father's family figure in *The Autumn Garden* and *Toys in the Attic*.

Max Hellman owned a shoe store on Canal Street until his partner absconded with the firm's funds, bankrupting him. When Miss Hellman was five, the family moved to New York to make a new start. They still spent six months of each year in New Orleans, but she attended New York's Wadleigh High School and, for three years, New York University. She also took some courses at Columbia. She has said that she started writing as a child, but the only juvenilia to see print was a high school column (titled after Heywood Broun's), "It Seems to Me, Jr."

After she left NYU she took a job as a reader for the publishing firm of Boni and Liveright. She also wrote book reviews for the New York *Herald Tribune*, read plays for Anne Nichols (*Abie's Irish Rose*), Harry Moses, and Leo Bulgakov, worked as publicist and subscription manager for a stock company in Rochester, New York, and was publicist for a Broadway show called *The Bunk of 1926*.

On December 31, 1925, Miss Hellman married Arthur Kober, then press agent for Jed Harris, later a successful playwright and screenwriter himself (*Having Wonderful Time*). The Kobers went to Paris, where he edited an English-language magazine, *The Paris Comet*, in which two of Miss Hellman's short stories appeared. Another story was published in a French magazine. Miss Hellman calls these early efforts "lady-writer stories."

After returning from Europe, she went to Hollywood in 1930 as a scenario reader. There she met Dashiell Hammett, her close friend and a strong influence on her life and work until his death in 1961. Hellman gives something of the day-of-the-locust atmosphere of the Hollywood of those days in *An Unfinished Woman*. She mentions a producer's speaking of his daughter's "perberty," a coinage she must have remembered when she wrote the short stories published in *The American Spectator*—"I Call Her Mama Now" and "Perberty in Los Angeles."

In 1932 Hellman divorced Arthur Kober and went to work as a play reader for Herman Shumlin, for whom she discovered *Grand Hotel*. She had earlier collaborated with Louis Kronenberger on a play, *Dear Queen*, but it was never produced.

While reading for Shumlin, Miss Hellman was working on *The Children's Hour*. In May 1934, she brought him two copies of the sixth draft, and they read it together. Shumlin said, "From the time I read it until the time it opened there weren't a dozen lines changed" (*Sun*, Jan. 18, 1936). Because of its "taboo" homo-erotic subject matter, well-known actresses were afraid to touch it, remembering the arrests of the actors who appeared in the New York production of *The Captive* only eight years before. A cast of virtual unknowns was finally assembled, and *The Children's Hour* opened November 20, 1934. Between the dark of November 20 and the daylight editions of the newspapers, Miss Hellman and her play became Broadway sensations, and *The Children's Hour* remained at the Maxine Elliott Theater for 691 performances, at that time the longest run in the history of that theater.

With the success of the play Miss Hellman's life changed abruptly. She had fifty-five dollars in the bank when *The Children's Hour* opened. She made approximately $125,000 from the production and spent it as fast as she made it. Reminiscing to an interviewer in 1952, she said, "I remember the surprise of its being a success . . . . I hadn't thought about that one way or another—I don't think I understood very much about the success or failure of plays in those days. And I was very pleased with the amount of the first week's royalties, and I bought presents—expensive luggage—for my friends, most of whom couldn't use it because they couldn't afford to travel" (*HT*, Dec. 14, 1952).

Although apparently enjoying her new celebrity, she didn't merely sit back and collect her royalty checks. She signed a four weeks' contract with Reliance Pictures while *The Children's Hour* was still running. Nothing came of the contract, but Samuel Goldwyn signed her, together with Mordaunt Shairp, author of *The Green Bay Tree*, to write the script for a remake of *The Dark Angel*.

Pleased with the success of *The Dark Angel*, Goldwyn bought the movie rights to *The Children's Hour* for fifty thousand dollars and hired Hellman to write the adaptation. (The producers of the 1962 film version paid $185,000 for those rights, none of which went to Hellman.) While in Hollywood, she worked on her second play, *Days to Come*, which opened on Broadway in 1936 and closed in a week. Miss Hellman said, "*Days to Come* was botched. The whole production was botched, including my botching. It was an absolute horror of a failure. I mean the curtain wasn't up ten minutes and catastrophe set in. It was just an awful failure. Mr. William Randolph Hearst caused a little excitement by getting up in the middle of the first act and leaving with his party of ten. I vomited in the back aisle. I did. I had to go home and change my clothes. I was drunk" (*WW*, p. 123).

While the failure of *Days to Come* may have shaken her confidence, it didn't leave her penniless because she was already committed to do the screen adaptation of *Dead End* for Goldwyn. When the script was finished, she sailed for Europe to visit France and Russia and to see the Spanish Civil War at first hand. She returned to America outraged at the atrocities she had seen in Spain. Walter Winchell asked her to write an article on her impressions for his column, but the Hearst papers refused to run it, calling her account "Loyalist propaganda." The article finally appeared in the *New Republic*.

With John Dos Passos, Archibald MacLeish, and Ernest Hemingway, Hellman formed Contemporary Historians, Inc. to have the celebrated director Joris Ivens film *The Spanish Earth*, a documentary of the Civil War, which was released in August 1937. She helped raise money for the Loyalist cause and for aid to Loyalist refugees and, as Hitler's armies moved through France, to European refugees from fascism.

Many forces in Hellman's life could have led her to support anti-fascist organizations. Perhaps it is as simple as a friend's explanation: "Lillian's politics grew roots when she was a kid. She once saw someone being pushed around and she's never gotten over it." [1] Most of her close friends were active in anti-fascist organizations—Nathanael West; his wife, "My Sister Eileen" McKenney; Hellman's producer, Herman Shumlin; and particularly her two closest friends, Dorothy Parker and Dashiell Hammett. Perhaps the most important and most immediate influence was the murder by the Nazis of her friend Julia, described in *Pentimento*. Hellman, whom *Time* described in 1952 as "the greatest meeting-goer in the world," worked with such organizations as the Friends of the Lincoln Brigade and the League of American Writers, with which Dashiell Hammett was actively involved.

Her political views touched off one of the theater's most colorful internecine quarrels when she and Tallulah Bankhead, star of Hellman's 1939 hit, *The Little Foxes*, disagreed about a benefit performance for Finnish relief. Miss Bankhead, as Richard Maney said, was apt to call anyone who disagreed with her politically a "dirty Communist." Refusing to allow the proposed benefit performance, Miss Hellman said, "I don't believe in that fine, lovable little Republic of Finland that everybody gets so weepy about. I've been there and it looks like a pro-Nazi little republic to me." Miss Bankhead ceased speaking to Miss Hellman. The feud was revived a few years later when Tallulah read that Hellman had purportedly said that "an actor doesn't make much difference to a play." She fired off her answer to the Letters department of *Time* magazine: "I loathe Lillian . . . a remark like that is beneath the contempt of an actor. . . . I'd like to see what some of her plays would be like with a second-rate cast." Miss Hellman, replying that she had been misquoted, continued, "Accustomed to yearly public greetings from the well-bred daughter of our plantation South I think the time has come to say that hate from Miss Bankhead is a small badge of honor, and praise undesirable. Miss Bankhead will never act in a play of mine again, only because I can stand only a certain amount of boredom." [2] There matters rested until the famous Truman Capote party two decades later, when Miss Hellman, moved by the memory of Tallulah's performance in *The Little Foxes*, made a gesture of reconciliation. The truce lasted only a year, however. When *The Little Foxes* was revived at Lincoln Center, Miss Hellman wrote an article for the *New York Times*, reminiscing about the first production. Tallulah contradicted Hellman's account in a letter to the *Times* and apparently carried her animus to the grave. Hellman had the last word in *Pentimento*.

As to Hellman's alleged left-wing views, she was consistently anti-totalitarian, and her views coincided with the Communist "Party line" only when that line became anti-fascist with changing Russian political maneuvers. For example, Miss Hellman was not a participant in the Fourth Writers Congress held in New York in June 1941, shortly before the German invasion of Russia. The Congress passed resolutions condemning our aid to European refugees and supporting the "peace-vigil" picket lines at the White House. Her absence indicates disagreement with the Congress's views, a disagreement made abundantly clear in *Watch on the Rhine*, which opened while the Nazi-Soviet Non-Aggression Pact was still in effect. (Albert Maltz asked in the *New Masses* (Feb. 12, 1946) why *Watch on the Rhine* was attacked as a play in 1941 while the film production was praised. The obvious answer was that "events had occurred during the interval" which changed the Party political stance. Maltz was reprimanded by the Party and forced to retract his criticism.)

In the late 1940s, as the congressional witch hunt began, Miss Hellman's outspokenness and membership in organizations labeled "Communist front" were to subject her to harassment and the loss of lucrative screen work, but in 1941 she adapted *The Little Foxes* as

an extremely successful movie. It was followed by the film version of
Watch on the Rhine.

As they had with *The Little Foxes*, people wondered whether any
of the characters in *Watch on the Rhine* were based on real people.
Miss Hellman told a reporter that the blackmailer in the play was
based on someone she had known, "one of the most glamourous
aristocrats in London . . . . I was invited to his house for supper,
although we had never met, and no sooner was dinner ended than I
found myself $700 out of pocket in one of the weirdest, crookedest
poker games in history" (*DN*, Apr. 28, 1941).

Her original screenplay *The North Star* was released in 1943. The
story of a Russian village during the days of the Nazi invasion, it was
highly praised at the time since the Russians were our allies. Later,
however, Adolphe Menjou cited the movie before the House
committee (HUAC) as an example of Communist propaganda. Miss
Hellman was unhappy with the final script as "prettified" by
director Lewis Milestone. She arranged for Viking Press to print her
original script and bought up her contract from Sam Goldwyn. She
never made another Goldwyn movie. (*The North Star* is occasionally shown on late-night television. It is now called *Armored Attack*,
and a prologue and epilogue have been added, consisting of
newsreel footage of uprisings against the Communists and a
voice-over with a "had-we-but-known" motif.)

II   *The Difficulties of the McCarthy Years*

The North Star and the 1946 film version of *The Searching Wind*
were to be her last movie scripts for twenty years. When Miss
Hellman and William Wyler planned to do *Sister Carrie* in 1948,
she discovered that she had been blacklisted by movie producers.
She was not removed from the blacklist until the 1960s. Readers too
young to remember this period might read Eric Bentley's *Thirty
Years of Treason*, Stefan Kanfer's *A Journal of the Plague Years*,
Walter Goodman's *The Committee*, and, of course, Hellman's own
Scoundrel Time. One got on the blacklist merely by having one's
name mentioned before the House of Representatives Un-American
Activities Committee. One got off the blacklist by being a "friendly
witness," giving other people's names to the committee.

Most witnesses were called before the House committee for
opinions held and actions performed back in the 1930s, when

intellectual and social ferment was in the air. Many were political innocents, like John Garfield, whose story Harold Clurman tells in *All People Are Famous*. Blacklisted and bewildered, Garfield waited for his attorney to get him a "clearance" from the committee; such a statement would allow him to work in the movies again. While Garfield's attorney was in a committee official's office, the phone rang. The man answered the phone, nodded, hung up and said, "The Garfield case is now closed. He just died of a heart attack. . . . He then added, 'Easy come, easy go.' The attorney struck him." Clifford Odets, who had named names before the committee, went in tears to Garfield's widow to say that he had been wrong to testify as he did.[3]

An interviewer asked Hellman years later whether she had been offered clearance if she "made an appropriate act of contrition." She said: "Later. Shortly after the first black-listing I was offered a contract by Columbia Pictures—a contract that I had always wanted—to direct, produce, and write, all three or any. And a great, great deal of money. But it came at the time of the famous movie conference of top Hollywood producers. They met to face the attacks of the Red-baiters and to appease them down. A new clause went into movie contracts. I no longer remember the legal phrases, but it was a lulu. I didn't sign the contract" (*WW*, p. 133).

Some remarks of hers, printed in *The Screen Writer* in December 1947, also surely did her no good with the producers, who were frantically trying to pacify the House committee: "Naturally, men scared to make pictures about the American Negro, men who have only in the last year allowed the word Jew to be spoken in a picture, who took more than ten years to make an anti-Fascist picture, these are frightened men and you pick frightened men to frighten first. . . . Judas goats, they'll lead the others, maybe, to the slaughter for you. The others will be the radio, the press, the publishers, the trade unions, the colleges, the scientists, the churches—all of us. All of us who believe in this lovely land and its freedoms and rights, and who wish to keep it good and make it better."[4]

Red Channels, a paperbound blacklist, was published for the convenience of radio, television, and movie producers. Mentioning this work and a similar one called *Counterattack*, Elmer Rice said, "It was pointed out that I was one of a group of 'leading playwrights' who had long 'front records.' Others named as members of this

group of Kremlin underlings were Clifford Odets, Lillian Hellman,
Marc Blitzstein, Garson Kanin, Arthur Miller, Arthur Laurents,
and Oscar Hammerstein II." [5]

In 1952 Miss Hellman was subpoenaed by the House committee.
Before her appearance she sent a letter that has often been quoted
to the chairman, Representative John S. Wood, Democrat, Geor-
gia, stating her position:

Dear Mr. Wood:

As you know, I am under subpoena to appear before your Committee on
May 21, 1952.

I am most willing to answer all questions about myself. I have nothing to
hide from your Committee and there is nothing in my life of which I am
ashamed. I have been advised by counsel that under the Fifth Amendment
I have a constitutional privilege to decline to answer any questions about
my political opinions, activities and associations, on the grounds of
self-incrimination. I do not wish to claim this privilege. I am ready and
willing to testify before the representatives of our Government as to my
own opinions and my own actions, regardless of any risks or consequences
to myself.

But I am advised by counsel that if I answer the Committee's questions
about myself, I must also answer questions about other people and that if I
refuse to do so, I can be cited for contempt. My counsel tells me that if I
answer questions about myself, I will have waived my rights under the Fifth
Amendment and could be forced legally to answer questions about others.
This is very difficult for a layman to understand. But there is one principle
that I do understand: I am not willing, now or in the future, to bring bad
trouble to people who, in my past association with them, were completely
innocent of any talk or any action that was disloyal or subversive. I do not
like subversion or disloyalty in any form and if I had ever seen any I would
have considered it my duty to have reported it to the proper authorities.
But to hurt innocent people whom I knew many years ago in order to save
myself is, to me, inhuman and indecent and dishonorable. I cannot and will
not cut my conscience to fit this year's fashions, even though I long ago
came to the conclusion that I was not a political person and could have no
comfortable place in any political group.

I was raised in an old-fashioned American tradition and there were
certain homely things that were taught to me: to try to tell the truth, not to
bear false witness, not to harm my neighbor, to be loyal to my country, and
so on. In general, I respected these ideals of Christian honor and did as well
with them as I knew how. It is my belief that you will agree with these
simple rules of human decency and will not expect me to violate the good
American tradition from which they spring. I would, therefore, like to come
before you and speak of myself.

I am prepared to waive the privilege against self-incrimination and to tell you anything you wish to know about my views or actions if your Committee will agree to refrain from asking me to name other people. If the Committee is unwilling to give me this assurance, I will be forced to plead the privilege of the Fifth Amendment at the hearing.

A reply to this letter would be appreciated.

Sincerely yours,
LILLIAN HELLMAN (*ST*, pp. 92–94)

Commenting on Miss Hellman's letter, Chairman Wood said that the committee would not allow a witness to dictate terms for testifying or appear to be "placed in the attitude of trading with the witnesses." [6]

Asked at the hearing whether she was acquainted with Martin Berkeley (screenwriter and ex-Communist who had named Miss Hellman as one of 160 Communists he had known in Hollywood), she stopped testifying. (She still has never met Martin Berkeley.) She had been subpoenaed because of Berkeley's testimony that Donald Ogden Stewart, Dorothy Parker, her husband, Alan Campbell, Dashiell Hammett, and Lillian Hellman were at a Hollywood organizational meeting. In a 1973 *Rolling Stone* interview, Ring Lardner, Jr., laughed when recalling Berkeley's testimony because, he said, he knew that the people named hadn't been there. He knew because he *had* been.

Asked about her testimony, Hellman said: "I think they knew I was innocent, but they were interested in other people. It was very common in those days, not only to talk about other people, but to make the talk as interesting as possible. Friendly witnesses, so-called, would often make their past more colorful than ever was the case. Otherwise you might turn out to be dull. I thought mine was a good position to take—I still think so" (*WW*, p. 127). Of the general reaction to McCarthyism, she said, "I was so unprepared for it all, so surprised McCarthy was happening in America. So few people fought, so few people spoke out. I think I was more surprised by that than I was by McCarthy. . . . Still painful to me, still puzzling" (*WW*, p. 133). Asked whether she had ever considered writing about that period, she said, "I've never known how to do it. It was really a clownish period. It was full of clowns talking their heads off, apologizing, inventing sins to apologize for. And other clowns, liberals, who just took to the hills. Ugly clowning is a hard thing to write about. Few people acted large enough for drama and not pleasant enough for comedy" (*WW*, p. 134).

The committee's question about her political affiliations was finally answered indirectly in *An Unfinished Woman*: "I do not wish to avoid the subject of Hammett's political beliefs, but the truth is that I do not know if he was a member of the Communist Party and I never asked him. . . . Once, in an argument with me, he said that of course a great deal about Communism worried him and always had and that when he found something better he intended to change his opinions. And then he said, 'Now please don't let's ever argue about it again because we're doing each other harm.' And so we did not argue again and I suppose that itself does a kind of harm or leaves a moat too large for crossing, but it was better than the arguments we had been having—they had started in the 1940s— when he knew that I could not go his way" (*UW*, pp. 263–64).

Eric Bentley, who in 1952–53 accused Hellman of writing an apologia for accused Communists in *The Children's Hour*, has finally decided that he was wrong. He says: "Miss Hellman, as we now know from her autobiography, *An Unfinished Woman* . . . never had been a Communist, but has related in private conversation with the editor of this book that her attorney became very nervous about her losing the 'privilege as to details' by disclosure of whatever she might disclose." The transcript of her testimony shows that, when asked whether she was a member of the Communist Party, Miss Hellman replied, "No, sir." She continued to say "No" until asked whether she had been a Party member five years before. Bentley explains that, "at this point, Miss Hellman relates, her attorney was kicking her so vigorously under the table that she answered, 'I must refuse to answer.' But Wood continued: 'Were you two years ago from this time?' And perhaps the kicking had subsided a little, for Miss Hellman answered, 'No, sir.' 'Three years ago from this time?' 'I must refuse to answer.' And thus it was, Miss Hellman says, that the report could circulate that she had left the Communist Party between two and three years earlier.

"This anecdote, if believed—and the present editor believes it—is interesting evidence of the way in which others than Party members did stand on the Fifth. It is also evidence of the terrible confusions of those years. . . . But most important—a landmark, actually—was the position taken by Miss Hellman in her letter. . . . The final irony was that, at a time when people, including some of her closest friends, were going to jail for far less, she got away with it. History isn't all bad." [7]

Although blacklisted by the movie industry through the late

1940s and 1950s, Hellman continued her unbroken string of Broadway successes with *The Searching Wind* (1944), an anti-appeasement play, and *Another Part of the Forest* (1946), depicting the early life of the Hubbards of *The Little Foxes*. Herman Shumlin had directed all her plays until *Another Part of the Forest*, which was produced by Kermit Bloomgarden and directed by Hellman herself.

In 1948 she went to Yugoslavia to attend the opening of *The Little Foxes* (Yugoslavian title, *The Grasshoppers*) at the National Theater in Belgrade. While there she interviewed Marshall Tito. A series of articles about her trip appeared in the *New York Star*. She also went to Paris, where French poet Phillipe Soupault took her to see Emmanuel Roblès' play *Montserrat*. She was so impressed with it that she asked Kermit Bloomgarden to get the American dramatic rights. She had been working on an adaptation of Norman Mailer's *The Naked and the Dead*, but dropped it when she decided that she was writing a completely new work. Hellman not only adapted *Montserrat* but also directed it.

After it opened to mixed reviews, she said, "I think 'Montserrat' is a good play and can't agree with those who don't. Not a great play, but a simple, honest play, and I can talk about it this way because it's not essentially mine" (*Sun*, Dec. 16, 1949). *Regina*, Marc Blitzstein's operatic version of *The Little Foxes*, also opened in 1949 to mixed notices. Miss Hellman said of it, "I like it very much. It's very impressive. . . . It took great courage and guts to do a show like that. . . . I almost meant 'The Little Foxes' to be a kind of dramatic comedy. Yes, I did" (*Sun*, Dec. 16, 1949).

In 1951 *The Autumn Garden*, her first original play in five years, drew good reviews but did average business. It is her favorite and, in many respects, her best play. Talking about the theme, she said, "I haven't been conscious of trying to do anything different. You change and what you do changes with it. . . . Perhaps, in the play, I've wanted to say that if you've had something to stand on inwardly when you reach the middle years you have a chance of being all right; if you haven't you just live out your life" (*WTS*, Mar. 3, 1951).

After her House appearance in 1952, Hellman directed a Broadway revival of *The Children's Hour*, to excellent reviews. As an indication of the changed financial situation in today's theater, Richard Maney compared the financial status of the original production and the revival: "The first production cost Herman Shumlin $10,000, the revival nicked Kermit Bloomgarden for

$35,000. In only one week did the original play do as much as $14,000. It averaged $11,500. On its reproduction at the Forrest, the stop clause was $14,000. In its twenty-three-week run there, business was as much as $21,000 in a week. But it didn't recover its cost. The original made a small fortune." [8]

Miss Hellman had bought a farm, Hardscrabble, with the profits from *The Little Foxes*. She and Hammett spent many happy hours there, and it was her real home until 1952, when, blacklisted and uncertain of future income, she had to sell it. There was not another Hellman play on Broadway until her 1955 adaptation of Anouilh's *The Lark*, starring Julie Harris. *The Lark* was followed by her adaptation in 1956 of Voltaire's *Candide*, for which Leonard Bernstein wrote the music and Richard Wilbur, lyrics. *Candide* was a box-office failure, which evidently disturbed her greatly. Asked whether she had enjoyed her adaptations, she said, "Sometimes, not always. . . . I got nothing but pain out of *Candide*" (*WW*, pp. 123–24). "In *Candide* I was persuaded to do what I didn't believe in, and I am no good at all at that game. It wasn't that the other people were necessarily wrong, I just couldn't do what they wanted. With age, I guess, I began to want to be agreeable (*WW*, p. 131).

Although there was no Hellman play on Broadway between *Candide* and *Toys in the Attic* in 1960, Hellman was not inactive. She formed a producing firm with Lester Osterman and encouraged novelists to write plays. Saul Bellow's *The Last Analysis* was a result.

In 1960 *Toys in the Attic* won the Drama Critics' Circle Award. The Pulitzer drama jury selected it for the drama award, but the board rejected the play and presented its award to *Fiorello!* Although Hellman's play was a critical and commercial success, 1960 and 1961 were years of great unhappiness for Miss Hellman. Dashiell Hammett, in poor health ever since his stay in prison (he had refused to give information to the House committee about the source of the bail funds for the Unfriendly Ten), died of lung cancer on January 10, 1961. Miss Hellman delivered the eulogy at his funeral service, calling him "a man of simple honor and great bravery." Speaking of his conviction for contempt of court, she said, "He didn't always think very well of the society we live in and yet when it punished him he made no complaint against it and had no anger about the punishment" (*HT*, Jan. 13, 1961). A veteran of both World Wars, Hammett was buried in Arlington Cemetery.

After Mr. Hammett's death, Miss Hellman was named executor

of his estate, which was insolvent because of tax claims. She and Arthur W. A. Cowan (subject of a fascinating chapter in *Pentimento*) bought the copyright interests of Hammett's estate for five thousand dollars. She wanted to republish some of his work, much of it long out of print. Now a new generation of readers is enjoying the reprints of *The Thin Man, The Maltese Falcon, The Glass Key,* and the short stories. *The Thin Man,* dedicated to Hellman and full of witty dialogue and inside jokes (she was the model for Nora Charles, the hero's intelligent but wacky wife; a minor character is recognizably Oscar Levant), gave rise to a series of highly successful movies starring William Powell and Myrna Loy. And, of course, *The Maltese Falcon* gave us the film classic starring Humphrey Bogart as Sam Spade. In the heyday of radio, the success of *The Thin Man* led Hammett to try a series featuring "The Fat Man."

III *Further Difficulties in New York and Hollywood*

A new movie version of *The Children's Hour* was released in 1962. The direction was heavy-handed and the casting a mistake, and the once-scandalous play, filmed under its own title, attracted little attention. Hellman's copy of the film script contains several notations in her handwriting—"Awful—L.H." The critics generally agreed with her. She said of the movie later, "They tried, but they botched it up. It was a dreadful film. I'm glad I had nothing to do with it" (WTS, May 21, 1964).

The film version in 1963 of *Toys in the Attic* turned excellent Hellman into bad Tennessee Williams. Dean Martin, as Julian, admitted that he never read the entire script, just his part. The script was rewritten to feature Geraldine Page. The part of one of the major characters was eviscerated to the degree that there was no apparent dramatic point to her presence in the movie; whole speeches were reassigned; the movie was given a "happy" ending, absent from the original; and again Miss Hellman received the criticism for a script she hadn't written.

Asked in 1962 whether she would consider doing an original screenplay, she said, "Sure I would. I think, as a matter of fact, you can make a very good case for pictures being a lot better than the theater these days, and I ain't crazy about pictures. I'm no movie buff, but I really hate snobbishness about pictures. They can be a lot of fun when they go right" (*HT*, Mar. 4, 1962).

Her experience with *The Chase* in 1965 changed her mind. She was hired to write a script for the film, her first movie job in twenty years. The indefinite article applies because she did not write *the* script, although her name appeared in the credits. Consequently, she was raked over the coals by critics who apparently had not read the *New York Times*, in which Peter Bart wrote:

In undertaking the script Lillian Hellman told friends she was intrigued by the prospect of dissecting a Texas town, in the light of the Kennedy assassination, to reveal the undercurrents of brutality. Though Miss Hellman now declines to comment on the film it is fairly common knowledge in Hollywood that she became distressed over the later hiring of Horton Foote to modify her script. Those associated with *The Chase* readily acknowledge that there have been abundant differences of opinion about the script and other matters (*NYT*, June 20, 1965).

Arthur Penn, the director, said, "Everybody had high hopes for it. Then the 'powers that be' felt that her script wasn't tight enough, so they brought in Horton Foote. They just wouldn't say, 'This is Lillian's script—let's go!' " (*NYT*, Feb. 13, 1966) Hellman told interviewer Irving Drutman, "Decision by democratic majority vote is a fine form of government, but it's a stinking way to create. So two other writers were called in, and that made four with Mr. Spiegel and Mr. Penn, and what was intended as a modest picture about some aimless people on an aimless Saturday night got hot and large, and all the younger ladies in it have three breasts, and—Well, it is far more painful to have your work mauled about and slicked up than to see it go in a wastebasket" (*NYT*, Feb. 27, 1966).

She became just as disillusioned about the theater. She said, "I used to like to go to the theater. . . . I find it hard to go now—most of it is so bad, so dull. . . . I don't understand about musicals now—very little good music, very little fun. . . . But then I don't understand about straight comedy, either—the audience laughs and I wish I could." Employing one of her favorite metaphors to describe the theater, she said that, in the theater as in painting, "the avant garde has met and embraced the Establishment. Now it's all just fashions" (*NYT*, Feb. 27, 1966). She called the New York audience "an expense account audience," apt to ignore any new play except "an occasional stylish success, which it can't help but go to because it must be informed about certain artistic matters for its own survival" ("Yale Reports" Radio Program, June 5, 1966).

The failure in 1963 of Hellman's last Broadway play, *My Mother,*

My Father and Me, was not responsible for her disillusionment with the theater, although it surely reinforced it. Of this failure she said, "It opened during the newspaper strike, and that was fatal. . . . I hope it will be revived because I like it. Off Broadway. I had wanted it done off-Broadway in the beginning" (*WW*, p. 124). She had been working on another play when she read the Burt Blechman novel *How Much?*—and wrote her adaptation instead. "It never occurred to me," she said, "that I wouldn't go back to it, but I haven't even read it again. . . . And it has nothing to do with failure. I began feeling this way before 'Toys in the Attic,' long before that. . . . I feel like a stranger in the theater now" (*NYT*, Feb. 27, 1966).

IV A New Career

Although inactive in the theater, she continued to teach and travel, writing several articles which may have led to her decision to write her memoirs.

She attended the International Drama Conference in Edinburgh: "The Drama Conference took place in McEwan Hall. Around the dome . . . run the words from Proverbs, 'Wisdom is the Principal Thing.' Maybe, but not that week" (*NYRB*, Oct. 17, 1963).

In 1963 she covered the Freedom March in Washington for the *Ladies' Home Journal*. In "Sophronia's Grandson Goes to Washington," mixed with the indictment of bigots and brutality and the description of the march are scenes from her childhood in New Orleans, centered around her childhood nurse and adult friend, Sophronia. Sophronia Mason was the first "cool teacher" Hellman always felt she needed, a role the nurse filled until her death. She figures largely in *An Unfinished Woman*, and her name appears in Hellman's plays more than once.

An attorney for a sheriff in Alabama asked that the *Journal* retract portions of Hellman's article. The magazine did so in the March 1964 issue, but just below the retraction was a statement by Miss Hellman: "My article, in all important matters, tells the truth and I wish to disassociate myself from the above retraction. What is true should not be obscured by the fear of lawsuits" (p. 82).

Hellman also covered the Pope's trip to Jerusalem in 1964 for the *Ladies' Home Journal*. The most memorable writing in "The Land That Holds the Legend of Our Lives" is not the journalistic reporting but the reminiscences of her childhood that were prompted by the trip. She might have been remembering her

troubles in the 1950s when she described her difficulties with the
Jordanian authorities. She was barred by Jordan because she was a
"well-known Zionist." She wrote in the April 1964 issue that the
barring "will amuse Zionists who used to say that I should be and
were angry that I wasn't. If you live long enough, people get around
to thinking you've been anything that suits their case against you on
the day they want the case against you" (p. 57).

In 1967 she went to Russia to refresh her memories for the book
then in preparation. Shortly after her return, Dorothy Parker, like
one of her own lost ladies, died alone in her hotel room. Lillian
Hellman delivered the eulogy at her funeral. Her chapter on Miss
Parker in *An Unfinished Woman* is, as a reviewer said, the only
work about her that gives more than it takes. (John Keats's
biography of Parker leans heavily on this chapter.)

In that same year *The Little Foxes* was triumphantly revived at
Lincoln Center, confirming its status as an American theater classic.
Elizabeth Hardwick, however, struck a dissenting note in a
peculiarly venomous review in the *New York Review of Books*
(Dec. 21, 1967). Hardwick none too subtly accused Hellman of
writing an "American version of Socialist Realism" and of pandering
to Broadway tastes: "And yet how wearying is the air in which *The
Little Foxes* drifts, the sky rich with stars, the earth voluptuous with
stuffs, the setting heavy and dark, pampered like some plum-plushy
whorehouse in which the girls are no longer young but ripe and
experienced in giving customer-satisfaction."

Hardwick's attack received quick response by such defenders as
Richard Poirier and Penelope Gilliatt. The late Edmund Wilson
wrote an open letter to Mike Nichols in the *New York Review of
Books* (Jan. 4, 1968) pointing out that "the very important respect in
which *The Little Foxes* is not old-fashioned is that Miss Hellman
does not only not feel under any obligation to write 'a tragedy with a
happy ending' but is not even aware of any necessity for calling her
play either a tragedy or a comedy." Hellman, however, has always
had trouble with literary ladies, Claire Booth Luce, Dorothy
Thompson, and Mary McCarthy, Edmund Wilson's ex-wife, among
them. In response to one of Miss McCarthy's digs, Hellman said
that Miss McCarthy is "often brilliant and sometimes even sound."
Hellman and Thompson clashed at a party given by Mrs. Luce.
Later in her 1940 Valentine's Day column, Miss Thompson
suggested "To the Communist Party of America—*The Little Foxes*."
Hellman had her revenge when Thompson called her about
adapting Thompson's play *Another Sun* for the movies.

Another Sun had run for eight performances in the season in which *Watch on the Rhine* won the Critics' Circle award. MGM had expressed interest in Thompson's play only if Hellman would adapt it. Thompson had sprinkled the dialogue with "local color" bits in German. When Thompson asked her about an adaptation, Hellman replied helpfully, "I suggest first that you translate it from the German." [9]

One lady who likes Hellman's work is playwright Jean Kerr, who said after seeing the revival of *The Little Foxes*, "I was so pleased. You know—you couldn't play the second act first. Isn't that nice? And you couldn't take out forty minutes and make it a lot better. . . . That's why I love to see the success of a shapely play—because I think it will encourage other people to write them. I like form, I like shape, I like design. . . . I like to think the playwright did *some* work before I got there." [10]

Through the 1960s and early 1970s Hellman continued to involve herself in political and intellectual causes she believed in. Perhaps most importantly, she was one of the organizers of the Committee for Public Justice, a group formed to prevent the excesses of the McCarthy era from being repeated. Representative Ichord (Mo.), chairman of the House Internal Security Committee (the renamed Un-American Activities Committee); singled her out for criticism, reviving the charges leveled against her in the fifties. Reading his accusations in the newspaper, anyone old enough to remember the fifties must have had a sense of *déjà vu*. In the light of Watergate, Miss Hellman's prescience in helping to form the Committee for Public Justice was equaled only by her courage.

As a prominent literary figure, Miss Hellman has accumulated many awards and honors, which culminated in the 1960s. She was elected to the American Academy of Arts and Sciences in 1960 and the American Academy of Arts and Letters in 1963, became vice-president of the National Institute of Arts and Letters in 1962 and was awarded in 1964 its Gold Medal (awarded only once every five years for "extraordinary distinction" in the arts). In 1961 she received an Achievement Award from Yeshiva University, the Brandeis University Creative Arts Award, and an honorary doctorate from Wheaton College. In 1968 she received an Award of Distinction from Tufts University. She also received honorary degrees from Yale University (1974) and Columbia University (1976) and was Regents' Professor at the University of California in Berkeley and Distinguished Professor at Hunter College. In 1975 she was named Woman of the Year by *Ladies' Home Journal* and

received the first annual Rappaport Prize awarded by Sarah
Lawrence College. In 1976 she won the MacDowell Award for
outstanding contributions to the arts.

Considering Hellman's age and long-time absence from the
theater, one might have considered these valedictory awards,
acknowledging the well-earned retirement of an eminent literary
figure. But, in addition to fulfilling teaching engagements at
Berkeley, Harvard, and Massachusetts Institute of Technology and
actively participating in the casting and rehearsal of *The Little
Foxes*, Hellman had embarked on a new career. In 1969 her memoir
An Unfinished Woman, appearing to glowing reviews and remaining on the best-seller lists for many weeks, won the National Book
Award. In 1973 *Pentimento*, its follow-up, became one of the few
examples of a sequel adjudged equal or superior to its predecessor.
Scoundrel Time, her story of the McCarthy era, appeared in 1976,
went into a second printing before publication, and received
superlative reviews.

In 1975 a gala benefit in Hellman's honor raised $35,000 for the
Committee for Public Justice, the civil liberties organization
Hellman helped found in 1970. Excerpts from her work were
performed at Circle in the Square Theater by such stars as Maureen
Stapleton and Jane Fonda. After the theater tribute Fonda led
Hellman on stage. Miss Hellman said that she thought tributes
came after death and she hoped that the evening's eulogies wouldn't
preclude a post-mortem memorial gathering. At a $100-a-plate
dinner at Gallagher's Hellman did her own star turn. Everybody
who was anybody was there: Jackie Onassis, Mike Nichols, Jean
Kennedy Smith, Carl Bernstein and Nora Ephron, Christopher
Plummer, Warren Beatty, Candy Bergen. The microphone went
dead as MIT President Jerome Wiesner began to speak, and the
diners babbled away. Hellman jumped up and told the guests to
shut up and be still. Leonard Bernstein considered that the high
point of the evening, "the old Lillian, the real Lillian, *au gratin*." [11]

As her "new career" continues and gains her a new audience, her
plays find a new audience also. In 1976 the revival of *The Autumn
Garden* at the Long Wharf Theater in New Haven received
excellent reviews. Also in 1976 Hellman received an offer of over
$500,000 from Universal for the rights to the memoirs, to be
combined into one Mike Nichols film. Hellman asked for the right
to approve the final cut. The studio refused, and Hellman dropped
the deal. She felt that she owed it to the friends she had written

about to see that their characters were not distorted. "After all," she said, "it's pieces of my life we're talking about. . . . My own life, after all, is more important to me than money. It is a question of moral responsibility" (*NYT*, Nov. 21, 1976).

Hellman may have refused the offer because of her experience with *Julia*. Although *Julia* was one of the major motion pictures of 1977-78 (all the principals involved were nominated for Academy Awards, and Jason Robards, Vanessa Redgrave, and screenwriter Alvin Sargent won Oscars), the controversy that seems inevitably to accompany Hellman swirled around the making of the film. Director Fred Zinneman had differences of opinion with her about the filming, and Hellman allegedly became upset with Jane Fonda (who portrayed Hellman) over some of Fonda's remarks in a *Newsweek* interview.

Hellman says that she thought the producers bought the story for the story itself, not because it was about her: "I know it's hard for anybody to believe me, but when I sold the rights to 'Julia,' it never occurred to me that my name would be used. I don't know why it didn't occur to me; it was very stupid of me. But there it is. The first I knew of it was when I read the script of the picture, when of course it was too late to say, I don't want my name used. They were—and are—perfectly within their rights to use it. But I would like to have seen my name changed. I don't want to be represented on the screen as me." [12]

Reviewers were almost too busy arguing about Hellman, or Fonda's activism, or Redgrave's socialism, to discuss the movie. Everyone agreed that *Julia* was visually beautiful. (A shot of a French railway station looked exactly like Monet's famous painting of the structure. Many scenes, in fact, looked liked Monets.) Some thought the script adhered too reverentially to Hellman's book. In a damaging way, it strayed too far from it. Former screenwriter Hellman's narrative is almost a shooting script; but the interminable childhood flashbacks which interrupt the action throughout the movie weaken the dramatic tension. Also the creators of the movie evidently thought all viewers would know a great deal more about Hellman and her friends than is likely; one doubts that some ever figured out who "Dottie" and "Ernest" were.

Some reviewers dealt with *Julia* as a feminist statement—or a failure to make one. It is natural, of course, that in the 1960s and '70s Hellman would be written about and interviewed concerning the new feminism. Erica Jong's protagonist in *Fear of Flying* considers and rejects Hellman as a "role model" because she "wants to be as much of a man as Dashiell Hammett so he'll love her like he loves himself." In *The Female Imagination*, Patricia Meyer Spacks discusses Hellman as a writer who both made students nervous and won their admiration. Whether or not Hellman serves as a role model for feminists, she could be one for men and women who want to learn how to grow up as they grow older. She defined wisdom for an interviewer: "I think it's the fitting together of things—the fitting together of people, knowledge, books, aims, all one knows and all one feels; fitting together as many of the pieces as you can." [13]

And so her readers and audiences await the next act in the life of Lillian Hellman, a wise and witty woman who, in her seventies, is in mid-career.

CHAPTER 2

The Plays of the 1930s

I The Children's Hour

Between the dark and the daylight,
  When the night is beginning to lower,
Comes a pause in the day's occupations,
  That is known as the Children's Hour.

—Longfellow

T HE place is Lancet, Massachusetts; the time, probably the 1930s. College friends Karen Wright and Martha Dobie have saved and struggled to found a successful girls' school. They are assisted, or rather hampered, by Martha's aunt, Lily Mortar, a retired actress. Their principal benefactress is rich Mrs. Amelia Tilford, whose maladjusted niece attends the school and whose nephew, Doctor Joseph Cardin, is engaged to Karen. Mrs. Tilford's influence has brought the daughters of her social set to the school.

Mary Tilford, the niece, building on overheard foolish remarks from Martha's aunt, lies to Mrs. Tilford so she will let the girl leave the school, where she has been punished for lying and other unpleasant behavior. The whispered lie is that Karen and Martha have a lesbian relationship. Confronted with the lie by the two teachers, Mary blackmails her schoolmate Rosalie into confirming it.

Mrs. Tilford phones her friends, who immediately remove their daughters from the school. The teachers sue for libel and lose, partly because Martha's aunt, who left to avoid the trouble, won't return to testify for them.

The two women, ostracized by the town, brood in the abandoned school until Martha tells Karen that there must have been an "ounce of truth" in the lie, that she may have loved Karen "that way." Karen rejects the suggestion. Martha goes to her room and shoots herself just before Mrs. Tilford arrives to announce that she has found out the truth and will make a public apology and financial restitution. Karen tells her that it is too late. Martha is dead and Karen has broken her engagement to Joe. Mrs. Tilford will have to live with the consequences of her hasty self-righteousness.

The stunning success of Hellman's first play was not an unmixed blessing. The extended publicity firmly fixed the "knee-jerk" critical stereotypes ever after associated with her work. Only one cliché is missing from the original reviews. Because Miss Hellman was not yet known as a critic of political and social wrongs, no one viewed the play as an indictment of the American way of life, although subsequent criticism made up for this oversight. At the time, John Howard Lawson actually criticized Hellman for *not* writing a social document: "The situation gives the impression of being implausible because it is not placed in a solid social framework. . . . The play ignores time and place. The prejudice against sexual abnormality varies. . . . We are given no data on this point." [1] And in "A Comparative Study of *The Children's Hour* and *Days to Come*" he complained that "the lack of unity in *The Children's Hour* derives from the author's inability to dramatize the social roots of the action. We are not shown the conditions in the environment which explain the little girl's demoniac hatred and the suffering of the two school teachers." [2] In later years, of course, it became customary to describe the play as a criticism of the rich and powerful, such comment ignoring the fact that even the giggling grocery boy persecutes the teachers.

The Children's Hour was kept before the public eye much longer than any other Hellman play, even longer than *The Little Foxes*, because of news articles about (1) its being banned in Boston, Chicago, and London; (2) the failure of the Pulitzer Prize committee even to attend a performance; and (3) the difficulties attendant on retitling and rewriting the film version to gain the approval of the Hays Office, the then-all-powerful Hollywood censorship board.

Producer Herman Shumlin planned a road tour with the original cast at the end of the Broadway run. Boston's Mayor Mansfield, who had not seen the play, threatened to take away the license of any Boston theater housing the production. He had also banned *Strange Interlude* and Sean O'Casey's *Within the Gates*. Shumlin sued the mayor and lost. Mayor Kelly of Chicago also banned the play. (The 1952 revival was again banned in Boston, but made it to Chicago, where the Cook County American Legion Anti-Subversion Committee urged civic, veteran, and school groups to boycott it because of Hellman's encounter with the House Un-American Activities Committee. The road production lost money, and the rest of the tour was cancelled.)

The necessity for clearing any public dramatic performance with the Lord Chamberlain, a law erased only in recent years, caused the London banning. Shumlin gained much newspaper space by offering to take the entire cast to England for one performance before the Lord Chamberlain in the hope of persuading him to change his mind. The play was finally performed in London in 1936 at The Gate, a private theater.

The Children's Hour was performed in Paris in 1936 under the title of *The Innocents*. French critics responded enthusiastically. Many discussed the significance of the locale, pointing out that, while New England Puritans might be shocked, in France no one would have cared.

If the censorship difficulties were not enough to make the most casual reader aware of the play, there was a minor flurry in the newspapers and weeklies when the Pulitzer drama award went to Zöe Akins' *The Old Maid*. It was widely rumored that William Lyon Phelps, the Grand Panjandrum of the drama committee, had refused to view a performance of *The Children's Hour*. Drama critics, incensed at the injustice, formed the Drama Critics' Circle, which ever since has awarded its own prize for the best Broadway play.

Finally, Sam Goldwyn, having bought the screen rights to *The Children's Hour*, was told by the Hays Office that he could neither use the title nor mention it in the advertising. Tentatively titled *The Night Is Beginning*, the movie was finally released as *These Three* with the plot "straightened out": the child says that she saw Martha in bed with Karen's fiancé. Thanks to the newspaper publicity given these details, the public, well aware that *These Three* was the famous *The Children's Hour*, flocked to see it, and it was one of the "top ten" pictures of the year.

Herman Shumlin had always considered the original title bad box office, arguing that the general public might miss the irony and think it a children's show. A New York *Herald Tribune* typesetter, thoroughly confused, captioned a picture of the movie's stars, Joel McCrea, Miriam Hopkins, and Merle Oberon, "These Those."

Of some minor interest at the time was the source of Hellman's plot, "Closed Doors; or, the Great Drumsheugh Case," a presumably factual account of a nineteenth-century trial published in

William Roughead's *Bad Companions*. Roughead reports the following story: The patroness of a girls' school placed her granddaughters there; one was Jane Cumming, black and illegitimate, "going seventeen." The two girls who supported her story were sixteen.

Marianne Woods, one of the teacher-partners, had been reared by her actress aunt, "whom she regarded as a mother" and who lived at the school. The other teacher, Jane Pirie, was "emotional and highly strung . . . irritable and petulant, apt to take offence, and as a friend very jealous and exacting." She and the aunt quarreled frequently.

Each teacher had a bedroom, shared by her pupils; in fact, each shared her bed with a pupil. Jane Cumming slept with Jane Pirie. Although Jane fawned on the teachers, she bitterly resented their strict discipline. She told her grandmother that they were homosexual. She then calmly returned to the school so that the teachers would suspect nothing while her grandmother was writing letters to her friends whose daughters attended the school. Within forty-eight hours they were all removed.

It was some time before the teachers could discover the cause. Having found out, they filed suit against the grandmother for £10,000. Although Jane was caught in lie after lie on the witness stand and the students and maid whom she cited as support for her story had obviously suspected nothing until Jane had filled their heads with her lies, the court found for the defendant. On appeal, the court found for the teachers. The case dragged on for ten years, with the teachers offering finally to settle for less than half. There is no record of the final outcome or of the eventual fates of the teachers or the girl.

Since certain inaccuracies concerning Hellman's alleged attitude toward her source seem in danger of being perpetuated, it might be well to clear up those inaccuracies. The most potentially damaging, because it appears in Richard Moody's work, the only previous book–length study of Miss Hellman, comes from Moody's apparent reliance on a Yale dissertation, in which the facts are, to say the least, scrambled. Moody writes that "neither the program, the advance notices, nor the published text, which appeared the day after the opening, indicated that the story was not original. John Mason Brown, in his New York *Post* review (November 21, 1934), was the first to refer to the source. A letter to the *Saturday Review* (March 16, 1935) reported that after the opening Miss Hellman said that the satanic 'imp came out of my own head.' She should have said that the imp came out of my own Roughead. But perhaps Miss Hellman doesn't like wise cracks." [3]

Mr. Moody's apparent source, unless the two men made the same errors independently, is John Brockington's doctoral dissertation, which argues the thesis that no woman can be a major playwright. Brockington says that "Miss Hellman's attitude towards her source is somewhat bewildering. There was no indication from her that *The Children's Hour* was anything but a purely original piece of work. However, it was *not long after the play opened* that her *unacknowledged indebtedness* was indicated in *a number of columns and letters* to the editor. . . . *When interviewed on the subject* Miss Hellman remarked," etc. [Italics mine]. The ordering of details implies that Miss Hellman, confronted with the statements in the columns, wormed her way out of a difficult situation, since he continues, "Surely the playwright was not naive enough to think that her source would not be uncovered. . . . We must therefore conclude that however conveniently Miss Hellman may have forgotten her source that [*sic*] we, in an attempt to study her play, should investigate it more thoroughly." [4]

Examining the original documents, one finds the following somewhat chronologically involved but, one trusts, accurate ordering of events.

Because of fear of censorship and police interference, *The Children's Hour* opened cold, without tryouts or publicity concerning the subject, on November 20, 1934. Mr. Brown's column of November 21, highly laudatory, did *not* mention the source. A Michel Mok interview with Miss Hellman appeared in the *Post* November 23. The opening paragraph of the interview reads: "It was the report of an eighteenth [*sic*] century Scottish law case that supplied the author of 'The Children's Hour' . . . with the germ for her plot." (Hellman had given Mok this information.) In his November 26 column, John Mason Brown referred to two letters from Earle Walbridge about *Bad Companions*. In the letter to the *Saturday Review* referred to by Moody, Mr. Walbridge mentioned the Brown column of the 26th, incorrectly stating that it appeared the day after *The Children's Hour* opened. In a reference to Mok's interview on the 23rd, Mr. Walbridge, again getting the date wrong, wrote, "Interviewed on the evening that the play opened, Miss Hellman, in answer to a question as to how she happened to conceive the character of the Satanic imp replied: 'The imp came out of my own head.' It is my suggestion that she should have said, 'The imp came out of my own Roughead.' "

The actual context of Hellman's "imp" remark was this: In answer to a question as to how she had conceived the character of the girl, where she had obtained her "almost clairvoyant insight into the workings of the child mind," Hellman said, "What I know about children I only know because I myself have been a child. The imp came out of my own head" (*Post*, Nov. 23, 1934).

One must conclude that Miss Hellman's fabled reputation for honesty remains intact.

Combining inaccuracies and further confusing dates, Babette Rosmond refers to a *New Yorker* review by Robert Benchley, mistakenly gives December 1, 1934, as the date of the opening night of *The Children's Hour*, and says, "Most people thought the play *was* fiction, and it's possible Miss Hellman may not have appreciated the fact that Benchley brought up the Drumsheugh matter in his *New Yorker* review. He didn't include her among his favorite people." [5] In his glowing review of *The Children's Hour*, Benchley called it "the season's dramatic high-water mark. A fine brave play" and added, " 'The Children's Hour' is possibly not for children, but for any grown-up adult with half a mind it is almost obligatory" (*NY*, Dec. 1, 1934, p. 36).

The 1952 revival of *The Children's Hour* also attracted a good deal of publicity because of Hellman's recent appearance before the House committee (HUAC) and the relevance of the play's theme to McCarthy-era character assassinations. In the 1930s the boldness of the subject matter had diverted critical attention from the true theme, although even then some critics understood it: Burns Mantle, for instance, said that "the true theme is the curse of scandalmongering and the whispering campaign, the kind of vicious lying that may easily wreck the lives of innocent persons." [6]

Hellman said of the revival, "There was less known about children in 1934 in a funny kind of a way and now the big lie is more fashionable. I've tried this time to take the emphasis off the child and make the play into the story of the two girls. . . . To my mind, the theme of Lesbianism is less this time and what comes out stronger is the power of a lie and what it can do to people when it has even one little ounce of truth" (*WTS*, Dec. 26, 1952).

In the 1950s critics understood the theme, spoke of its contemporary pertinence, and sometimes applied it specifically to the McCarthy witch hunt. They used such phrases as the "brutal impact of false testimony"; "exposure of the evils of character assassination"; "an impelling psychological story of the havoc a lie can cause." Brooks Atkinson thought that the play "might have grown a bit in stature" since we have learned that "lives can be destroyed by other types of slander. Having been intelligently written for the values of 1934, 'The Children's Hour' fits the world of today just as accurately."

Atkinson had objected to the last ten minutes in the original production as unnecessary. He still found "those last ten minutes or so of retribution . . . a little overwritten," adding "Miss Hellman insists upon saying some things that are superfluous in the stunned atmosphere of her summing-up. But not many things. She needs that final twist of the dagger. She is entitled to show that the slanderer is doomed as thoroughly as those who have been slandered, and that righteousness is a ruthless form of vanity and that there is no way of undoing a wrong committed out of a sanctimonious attitude" (*NYT*, Dec. 19, 1952).

Eric Bentley, no friend of American drama or of Hellman, reviewed the play in the *New Republic* (Jan. 5, 1953) as a deliberate defense of Communism. Like the farmer in Robert Frost's "Mending Wall," he liked having thought of the notion so well he repeated it in *The Dramatic Event* and again in *American Drama and Its Critics*: "We are told that the play has been revived because of the current red scare. . . . The political analogy suggests not only the logical weakness of Miss Hellman's position but also the historical and psychological path along which she reached it. Is it not in politics, rather than the theatre, that we have witnessed this drama before? . . . *The Children's Hour* has nothing directly to do with communism, but it was written in the thirties, and is the product of the dubious idealism of that time." [7]

In "The American Drama 1944–1954," Bentley returns to the attack on Hellman: "Another habit of the quasi-liberal mind has been to say that of course so and so is not a communist and yet, when it turns out that so and so is or was a communist, to register no dismay, not even surprise. Of course he wasn't a communist, but, if he was, so what? This ambiguity has been given rather powerful expression by Lillian Hellman in *The Children's Hour* which was revived in the 1952–53 season with changes expressly calculated to suggest the play's relevance to McCarthyism. . . . *The Children's Hour* represent[s] a type of liberalism that has been dangerous and is now obsolescent." [8]

A comparison of the 1934 and 1952 texts of *The Children's Hour* fails to reveal the "expressly calculated changes" Mr. Bentley found. Deletions far outnumber additions, and all changes are minor. And, of course, Mr. Bentley has changed his mind about Hellman's politics.

Perhaps the late John Gassner, the finest critic of American drama in our time, might have the last word: "Although it is not difficult to discover the flaws in this work, a critic must develop a special resolve to denigrate American drama before he can resist the power of THE CHILDREN'S HOUR, especially in the throbbing second act. . . . We may view with some perturbation the fact that the plays written in recent years have so rarely possessed the power that belongs to THE CHILDREN'S HOUR." [9]

Because of the undue weight given the play in the Hellman canon by publicity and controversy, Hellman's later work has been forced to fit the image created by *The Children's Hour*. It is as if Arthur Miller's and Tennessee Williams' subsequent work were to be reviewed as extensions of *The Man Who Had All the Luck* and *Battle of Angels*. *The Children's Hour* is, after all, a first play, and should be examined as such. It has been consistently praised for its dialogue and its characterization. Certainly, by comparison with plays of the thirties and even with many later American dramas, it deserves this praise. But, if one looks at Hellman's later plays, particularly the three generally judged, in addition to *The Children's Hour*, as being her best (*The Little Foxes, The Autumn Garden, Toys in the Attic*), it is not a typical Hellman play.

A characteristic of later Hellman dialogue is that the rhythm and diction of a character's speeches fit that particular character. No one else in *The Little Foxes* talks like Birdie; Oscar is less intelligent than Ben and his talk shows it. Rose Griggs of *The Autumn Garden* is memorable for her *non sequiturs* and antecedentless pronouns. The grandmother in the same play, with her dowager wit, is individualized. The three older men are carefully differentiated— General Griggs's resigned seriousness, Crossman's rueful wit, Nick's lightweight, tinkering malice. In *Toys in the Attic* the surface softness of the one sister, the genuine love of the other are established through dialogue.

At its best, Hellman's dialogue is poetry of the theater, a quality not often appreciated in her work. As evidence, read the script of *Regina*, the operatic version of *The Little Foxes*, where Blitzstein's lyrics, following Hellman's dialogue, seem prosaic by comparison.

But *The Children's Hour* gives us only the beginning of this technique. There is little difference in the rhythm, diction, speech patterns of Karen and Martha or, for that matter, Joe, the fiancé. The grandmother does speak with an authority anticipatory of Mrs. Farrelly in *Watch on the Rhine* and Mrs. Ellis in *The Autumn Garden*, but she remains a type rather than an individual. With the exceptions of the child, Mary, and the old actress, Lily Mortar, there is little concrete detail in the characters' speeches.

Since it is a dramatic truism that characters are developed by what they say and do and what is said about them, one arrives at an explanation of why the lying child walked off with the play (and why the actress aunt is the second most memorable character). The comments of Brooks Atkinson and Joseph Wood Krutch at the time of the original production are typical of critical and audience reaction to the child. Atkinson wrote: "Miss Hellman has drawn the character of Mary so brilliantly that she almost throws her play off balance. Once Mary comes into it with a petty lie on her lips she dominates two acts of it with her plots and inverted craft and her mad dissembling. She is a miniature genius of wickedness" (*NYT*, Dec. 2, 1934). And, in the same vein, Krutch commented in the *Nation* (Dec. 5, 1934) that "the whole of the dramatic interest is centered upon the perverse child, and the only real concern of the audience is with her. At this point, however, [the end of the second act] she completely disappears from the play. . . . The character unceremoniously dropped is incomparably the realest and most vivid person in the play. . . . Moreover, all the real tension has developed around her" (p. 657).

At the time of the revival Hellman said about Mary, "On the stage a person is twice as villainous as, say, in a novel. When I read that story I thought of the child as neurotic, sly, but not the utterly malignant creature which playgoers see in her. I never see characters as monstrously as the audiences do—in her case I saw her as a bad character but never outside life. It's the results of her lie that make her so dreadful—this is really not a play about lesbianism, but about a lie. The bigger the lie the better, as always" (*NYT*, Dec. 14, 1952).

How does it happen that, as some critics felt, Mary is the center of the play? Returning to the examination of the dialogue, one finds that her speeches are unlike those of anyone else in the play. She is established as a liar and a bully by concrete dialogue about a missing bracelet and allowance money and a broken vase and wilted flowers and a specific book read furtively. The concrete dialogue is reinforced by concrete actions: arm-twisting, a fake heart attack. And, just as important for her characterization, when she is offstage during the first two acts she still dominates the play because the other characters talk *about* her.

In a minor way, the same devices of characterization are used for Lily Mortar. Both she and Mary are established immediately for us, Aunt Lily through her recitation and fatuous remarks to the girls, Mary through her entrance with the wilted flowers and subsequent stubborn defense of her lie. Aunt Lily's references to her past glories as an actress, to Sir Henry Irving, to the Infant Phenomenon, to the toilet backstage in Rochester, give us a concrete image of her character. And, like Mary, when she is offstage she is the subject of discussion between the two teacher friends.

The teachers' characterizations, on the other hand, are built more slowly, and most of their conversation tells us more about Mary and Aunt Lily than it does about the teachers themselves, but the teachers, too, finally become realized characters for us in that much-criticized third act. Many contemporary reviewers called this act too long, even unnecessary, some arguing that the play should have ended with Martha's suicide. This criticism apparently half convinced Miss Hellman, who wrote: "The play probably should have ended with Martha's suicide: the last scene is tense and over-burdened. I knew this at the time, but I could not help myself. I am a moral writer, often too moral a writer, and I cannot avoid, it seems, that last summing-up. I think that is only a mistake when it fails to achieve its purpose, and I would rather make the attempt, and fail, than fail to make the attempt." [10]

But should the play end sooner than it does? To begin with, it is in the last act, before Martha's suicide, that we finally see the two teachers as individuals, talking not about Aunt Lily or Mary but about themselves, their lives and their feelings, a development indirectly acknowledged by the frequent critical praise of the writing in the last act, particularly the dialogue between Karen and Martha and Karen and Mrs. Tilford. Oddly, these scenes are sometimes praised by the same critics who argue that they shouldn't exist.

But the real justification for that third act lies in an application of Francis Fergusson's discussion of dramatic rhythm in *The Idea of a Theatre*. He identifies the movements of a realistic play as being from purpose to suffering to new insight, with the protagonist on a search for his "true human condition," with the end of the quest an understanding of the past brought up in the light of present action. Examining Ibsen's *Ghosts*, Fergusson finds this rhythm truncated by its abrupt ending, with acceptance of the catastrophe lacking. The ending of *The Children's Hour* prevents a similar truncation. Martha's suicide is the end of *her* quest, but Karen and Mrs. Tilford must acquire new insight as a result of that suicide. Thus, with the final scene, the acceptance is there and the rhythm complete.

Hellman couldn't avoid that last summing up because it was necessary, necessary to a play written in the tradition of the Ibsen realistic drama. The latter statement brings us full circle to the thesis that *The Children's Hour* is in many ways an atypical Hellman play and anticipates what we shall find when we view her major plays: Lillian Hellman does not thereafter write in the Ibsen tradition, although many reviewers have thought so. The later plays *do* avoid that last summing up because they grow out of another tradition altogether, that of the novel, and employ the techniques of irony.

If, structurally, the last act is completely necessary, why did many of the reviews of the original production comment that Hellman seemed to change purpose in midstream, that the third act seemed anti-climactic though well-written? Misled by the impact in the theater of the Mary-centered dialogue, they misunderstood the playwright's purpose. The play is not about a psychopathic child or about lesbianism as subject or theme. The subject is character assassination; the theme is the damage done in our world by so-called "good" people, through self-righteous judgment, selfishness, blindness to their own weaknesses. The havoc is created, not by Mary's lie, but by adult reaction to it, even, finally, that of good old Joe, whose doubt topples the last domino. His doubt is the last in a chain of events causing Martha's suicide. Once the child's lie is released on the world, the liar ceases to matter.

In order to show the harm done, the teachers must be victims, again giving the theatrical impact to Mary. When a character is actively exerting his will, "plotting," it is human nature to get involved with him. The fact that Mary is the active character, coupled with the fact that the teacher's dialogue carries the exposition and characterization of other characters without telling us enough about the inner life of the teachers themselves, causes the

"let-down" feeling in the theater when Mary exits for the last time.
But, to end the play differently, with the suicide, say, although it
might have been Broadway wise, would have been thematically
dishonest.

Critics found less structural disharmony in the revival; perhaps
the minor cuts and rewriting, which tended to substitute the
concrete for the abstract, accomplished Hellman's intended change
of emphasis. Although some reviewers criticized Hellman the
director for pacing the last act too slowly, few criticized the last act
per se. John McClain said, "There is a memorable scene between
the grandmother and one of the stricken teachers which should be
recommended to all writers who believe a speech should run two
lines or not at all" (*JA*, Dec. 19, 1952). In a 1972 edition of her
Collected Plays, Hellman returned essentially, with minor deletions
and virtually no additions, to the 1934 script.

Looking at *The Children's Hour* some forty years after its original
production, one finds a flawed but still powerful play, indeed a
remarkable play for a beginning playwright. *The Children's Hour*,
though a first effort, revealed Hellman's ability to tell a story. And,
of course, that gift is a major reason for the survival of the play.
Critics who tried unsuccessfully to fit Hellman into the mold of the
social protest playwrights of the 1930s forget that, as Hellman said,
The Children's Hour "isn't about a time or a movement. It's a story"
(*NYT*, Dec. 14, 1952).

It also is an example of her consistent (and misunderstood) effort
to go beyond the limitations of the realistic form. Hellman has been
charged with writing melodrama and the well-made play (a
much-used, but much misunderstood term. After all, *Oedipus Rex*
is a well-made play). Examination of Hellman's works will show that
she attempted a form which, for lack of a better term, can be called
stylized realism. This technique, perfected in *The Little Foxes* and
Toys in the Attic, had its beginnings in *The Children's Hour*, still a
memorable contribution to the American theater. What a reviewer
wrote in 1953 is still true of the play in the 1970s: "What I should
like to underline . . . is the immense *theatricality* of the work—
the sheer, exhilarating sense it conveys of a positive dramatic talent,
of a playwright who is not afraid to calculate her exits and entrances,
to drop her curtains at a provocative moment, or to expose her
characters to passion and violence. It is this imaginative boldness
which has carried Miss Hellman past the failures of realism to a
secure and irreproachable ground." [11]

II Days to Come

For there is no remembrance of the wise more than of the fool for ever;
seeing that which now is in the days to come shall all be forgotten. And how
dieth the wise man? As the fool.—Ecclesiastes II, 16

The place is Callom, Ohio, two hundred miles from Cleveland;
the time, the 1930s. Andrew Rodman, a paternalistic small-town
factory owner, is forced by lawyer Henry Ellicott (who owns
controlling stock in the company in return for money loaned to
Rodman) to call in strikebreakers to force his striking workers back
on the job. The workers are fond of their employer but unable to
live on Depression wages. Rodman's wife Julie, a restless woman,
full of purposeless energy, falls in love with Leo Whalen, a labor
organizer who has come to town to aid the strikers. One of the
imported gangsters kills a cohort and dumps the body at the labor
organizer's door. Whalen is arrested long enough for the hoods to
incite the workers to violence so they can defeat them.

Whalen is released when Julie Rodman provides him with an alibi
by revealing that she was with him when the body was dumped. In
the last scene she confesses to her husband that she has had an affair
with Ellicott. Rodman confesses in turn that he has borrowed
money from Ellicott to pay her extravagant bills. Cora Rodman,
Andrew's sister, made the loan necessary by refusing her brother a
loan, although she had money.

The strikers go back to work, but the "familial" feelings are gone,
both in the household and in the community.

The script has the ingredients of many successful 1930s plays and
movies. Hellman may, in fact, have been influenced by her movie
work. Unless the play is revived, one can only speculate on how
much of the failure lies in script weaknesses, how much in the
production. Hellman said of the latter, "The carefully rehearsed
light cues worked as if they were meant for another play; the props,
not too complicated, showed up where nobody had ever seen them
before and broke, or didn't break, with the malice of animated
beings; good actors knew by the first twenty minutes they had lost
the audience and thus became bad actors; the audience, maybe
friendly as it came in, was soon restless and uncomfortable. The air
of a theatre is unmistakable: things go well or they do not. They did
not" (*P*, p. 162).

Surprisingly, radical critics disliked the one Hellman play with obviously topical social subject matter. Charles E. Dexter (*Daily Worker*) and Alexander Taylor (*New Masses*) thought there was too much emphasis on—and too much sympathy with—the middle class. John Howard Lawson complained in *New Theatre and Film* that the labor organizer advises the workers to take no action and that "this is bad tactics." He concluded that Hellman's major fault lay in not being a Marxist: "Art cannot be created out of shreds and patches of beliefs and sentiments. One cannot interpret a living social process without a living social philosophy" (p. 61).

Hellman had said that the play centered on the family, with the strike and social conflicts as background: "It's a story of innocent people on both sides who are drawn into conflict and events far beyond their comprehension. It's the saga of a man who started something he cannot stop, a parallel among adults to what I did with children in 'The Children's Hour' " (*HT*, Dec. 13, 1936).

The faithful worker, Firth, may remind one of the feudal loyalty of Chekhov's Firs. If the reader of *Days to Come* finds the benevolent paternalism of the owner and the unquestioning loyalty of Firth unrealistic, he should study the history of union organizing in the South. When, after World War II, a CIO organizer came belatedly to a small East Texas town (the "Charity" of William Goyen's *House of Breath*) to organize the sawmill workers, he was bewildered and exasperated by the attitude of the striking workers. The secretary to the president of the lumber company had to cross the so-called picket line every morning. The line parted like the Red Sea, as the men took off their caps, said "Mornin', Miss Margaret," and waved her through. The men, although talked into organizing, were unenthusiastic because they lived in company houses with utilities paid and bought their necessities at the company sto'. Even though they often owed their souls to it, they remembered that no one had been laid off during the Depression; the mill owner, when banks collapsed and there was no money with which to pay the men, paid them in scrip good at the store. They never forgot it, even when they had so little left over on Friday pay days after their store bills were deducted that they could say, as one man did, "It may be pay day for some folks, but it's just Friday to me." In *Days to Come*, only a murder can break the ties of sentiment and tradition that bind the owner and his workers.

Although Hellman said the play was about individuals, most critics felt that the strike was the story and saw no connection between the strike and the revelation of the personal lives of the characters. Hellman attempted to develop a theme common to all her plays, that the world we live in is the sum total of the acts of each individual in it. Ignorance, dishonesty, and cowardice in personal lives affect social events. If the factory owner and his wife had understood their own motives, had been honest in their marriage, then he would not have been in the financial clutches of the lawyer and would not have been forced to call in the strikebreakers. If the owner's sister had not been selfish and greedy, Rodman could have used her money instead of borrowing from the lawyer.

Although reviewers saw no connection between this play and *The Children's Hour*, there is a continuity of theme. In an early version of the latter play, Mrs. Tilford says, "Mrs. Mortar, you are not innocent. We are both guilty, as guilty as if we had pulled the trigger ourselves. And so is the judge and jury . . . the newspapers, and yes, the church too." Although no such explicit statement remains in the final version, one sees in the events of *The Children's Hour* that no one person causes the tragedy; each bears a responsibility.

Even those critics who understood Hellman's purpose in *Days to Come* felt that she had one story too many. Burns Mantle, perhaps the most sympathetic critic, said, "Her tragedy is the tragedy of misunderstanding humans who find themselves in a pitiful impasse to which the strike and its theatrical factors were no more than incidental contributors. The situation of a feudal family of small-town America facing a strike and having its smug souls stripped by the experiences that follow is a sound dramatic foundation. The forcing of the abortive romance is less convincing, and it is on that rock the drama splits" (*DN*, Dec. 16, 1936). Hellman was attempting a technique which she later mastered, attempting to show more sides of a character than the drama normally reveals. (Several reviewers called the play novelistic. Hellman has always insisted that she has been influenced by novelists, such as Henry James, Stendhal, and Dickens, rather than by dramatists. She says that producer Kermit Bloomgarden insisted that she writes novels that are then transferred to the stage.)

Hellman has puzzled over the reasons for the failure of the play, suggests some of them in the Introduction to *Six Plays*, but concludes: "But with all that is wrong, all the confusion, the jumble, the attempt to do too much, I stand on the side of 'Days to Come.' I am only sorry that the confusion in the script confused the best director in the theatre, who, in turn, managed to confuse one of its most inadequate casts. . . . It was my fault, I suppose, that it happened. I do not believe actors break plays, or make them, either. And nothing would have affected the play if I had done what the writer must do: kick and fight his way through until the whole is good, and the audience will not stop to worry about the parts" (pp. ix-x).

In 1941, contemplating a series of matinee performances of *Days to Come* to run concurrently with *Watch on the Rhine*, Hellman said that she felt the elimination of one character, maybe the villain, would have made the play all right. The most criticized plot element was the thread of the wife's love for the labor organizer; the most criticized scene, that in which she confesses her feelings to him. Removal of that element might sharpen the focus of the play. Whalen, the labor organizer, functions almost as a commentator. With the sketchy romance removed, Hellman would have had more space to develop the family conflict.

The criticized scene is honestly written, but Hellman made what may have been a mistake dramatically. She drew more obviously on her own feelings than she was ever to do again. We know from her memoirs that she felt she was a learner, not a teacher, and that she needed the right teacher, a "cool teacher." Julie says to Whalen, "When I was young, I guess I was looking for something I could do. Then for something I could be. Finally, just for something to want, or to think, or to believe in. I always wanted somebody to show me the way. . . . I decided a long time ago that there were people who had to learn from other people. I'm one of them."

One of Hellman's strong qualities is the ability to enter into characters' lives with great understanding, but Julie is an imperfectly realized character, and in this one scene we may have, not Julie talking to Whalen, but Hellman to Hammett.

This scene and the third act, heavily cut, are much tighter in the definitive edition of the plays. The script is of interest to the student of Hellman's work because of the attempt to enlarge the boundaries of the realistic play and because of the clearer delineation of a major Hellman theme: "All the things we knew about each other, all the things that accumulate through a lifetime . . . sat quietly, waiting for us, while we lived politely and tried, like most people, to push them out of sight. Polite and blind, we lived. . . . All the things we know, were there to know a long time ago." (Act III) This speech is a variation of a theme in *The Children's Hour*: "There's something in you, and you don't know it and you don't do anything about it. Suddenly a child gets bored and lies—and there you are, seeing it for the first time. . . . In some way I've ruined your life. I've ruined my own. I didn't even *know*." (Act III) We find that theme again in *The Searching Wind*, the play most like *Days to Come* in structure, as Hellman shows us the cause-effect relationship between the characters' lives and the public events of their time: "You know, when you don't think you're bad, then you have a hard time seeing you did things for a bad reason, and you fool yourself that way. . . . maybe the hardest thing in the world is to see yourself straight" (Act II, Scene 3).

In *Days to Come*, as in *The Children's Hour*, *The Searching Wind*, *The Autumn Garden*, *Toys in the Attic*, the harm is done, not by a "villain," but by well-intentioned, self-deluded people.

Though flawed and tantalizing in the sketchy glimpses of the Rodmans it gives us, *Days to Come* is an interesting play. Hellman seems to like it better than *The Searching Wind*, a box office success. In *Pentimento* she says that, reading *Days To Come* again, she liked it: "it is crowded and overwrought, but it is a good report of rich liberals in the 1930's, of a labor leader who saw through them, of a modern lost lady, and has in it a correct prediction of how conservative the American labor movement was to become" (p. 163). Drama critic John Gassner, looking back in the 1940s, felt that *Days to Come* deserved better of New York than the fate it received.

III   The Little Foxes

Take us the foxes, the little foxes, that spoil the vines, for our vines have tender grapes.

—*Song of Solomon*, II, 15

The place is a "small town in the deep South"; the time, the spring of 1900. Regina Giddens and her brothers Oscar and Ben Hubbard plan to build a cotton factory in partnership with Mr. Marshall, a Chicago businessman. They are awaiting a response from Regina's husband Horace, who is being treated at Johns Hopkins for heart trouble, about putting up one-third of the money. When the brothers pressure Regina, she sends her daughter Alexandra to Baltimore to bring Horace home. She bargains with the brothers for a larger share. She and Ben agree that it will come from Oscar's share. When Oscar objects, they suggest to him that Alexandra may marry his son Leo. Birdie, Oscar's faded-aristocrat wife whom Oscar married for the cotton and the land, overhears.

Horace comes home and is filled in on the Hubbard machinations by faithful servant Addie. He refuses to give Regina the money. Unbeknownst to Regina, Leo takes Horace's railroad bonds from his deposit box for collateral for Marshall. Horace discovers the theft but prevents Regina's getting the upper hand by telling her he will say he lent the bonds to the Hubbard brothers. Regina will get only the bonds in his will.

Regina taunts him into a heart attack and lets him die trying to get to his medicine. She then confronts her brothers with the theft and threatens to send them to jail unless she gets the lion's share of the new business. She apparently wins, but at the end of the play Alexandra wonders aloud why her "poppa" was found on the stairs, and the shrewd Ben looks interested. Alexandra tells Regina she is leaving as the curtain descends on Regina climbing the stairs alone.

The Little Foxes has been Hellman's most continually performed play, a frequent choice of little-theater and summer stock groups. The sell-out six-weeks revival at Lincoln Center in 1967 was followed by a limited Broadway engagement. Probably the most popular of her plays and the one receiving the most acclaim from the critics, it is not Hellman's favorite. She says in *Pentimento* that it was her most difficult play to write, partly because of the failure of *Days to Come*, but, more importantly, because it had a "distant connection" to her mother's family.

Her mixed feelings about *The Little Foxes* may stem from her puzzlement at the critics' reactions to the play. It must be bewildering to be both praised and damned for the wrong reasons. She says, "I wanted, I needed an interesting critical mind to tell what I had done beyond the limited amount I could see for myself. But the high praise and the reservations seemed to me stale stuff and I think were one of the reasons the great success of the play sent me into a wasteful, ridiculous depression. I sat drinking for months after the play opened trying to figure out what I had wanted to say and why some of it got lost" (*P*, pp. 179–80).

Hellman must have been bemused to discover that nothing in the contemporary reviews or in the later analyses in book form indicates that audiences found *The Little Foxes* extremely funny. On the contrary, reviewers used words like "grim," "mordant," and "morbid" to describe the tone of the play. One reviewer even found actress Patricia Collinge, in the role of Birdie, guilty of "attracting laughs where none were intended." What was Miss Hellman's intention? She said, "I almost meant *The Little Foxes* to be a kind of dramatic comedy. Yes, I did," (*Sun*, Dec. 16, 1949) and thought Regina "kind of funny." "I think most villains are funny," she added. Hellman also thought Birdie "kind of silly" and added, "I just meant her to be a lost drunk. I was amazed to find much about *The Little Foxes* that I hadn't intended—aristocracy against the middle class and so on."[12] She said that in Alexandra, Regina's daughter, she meant to "half-mock [her] own youthful high-class innocence" and that she "had meant people to smile at, and to sympathize with, the sad, weak Birdie," adding, "Certainly I had not meant them to cry" (*P*, p. 180).

What of the Hubbards, whom critics, guided by the metaphorical title, described as wolves, eagles, and rats? Hellman writes, "I had meant the audience to recognize some part of themselves in the money-dominated Hubbards; I had not meant people to think of them as villains to whom they had no connection" (*P*, p. 180).

The Hubbards are based on real people. Outspoken on public issues but reticent about her family while her relatives were living, Hellman said at the time of the original production only that some people thought it was her mother's family. With the publication of *Pentimento* readers learned that the Hubbards were indeed inspired by her mother's family, wealthy Southerners who had left Alabama to go North, where the money was. Hellman says that in her late teens she "began to think that greed and the cheating that is its usual companion were comic as well as evil" and "began to like the family dinners with the talk of who did what to whom" (p. 181).

Attempting to portray the Hubbards as she saw them, as both "sinister and comic," to use John Gassner's phrase, Hellman used irony, a quality which calls for an objective, amused detachment, a hallmark of Hellman plays, which, to borrow from Gassner again, American audiences don't understand or like.

Two women leaving Lincoln Center after seeing *The Little Foxes* were overheard discussing the performance with great animation. One woman checked herself in mid-praise, saying, "Well, of course, it's just a melodrama." Add to that term the phrase "well-made play," and one has the history of the criticism of *The Little Foxes*. When one thinks of melodrama, one thinks of a play with artificially heightened emotion; stereotyped, unindividualized characters given to unmotivatd fifth-act conversions; and improbable turns of plot leading to a conventionally happy ending, with vice punished and virtue rewarded. The Hellman play does not fit the definition. Certainly Hellman uses devices associated with melodrama—stolen bonds, threats, blackmail. But to what purpose? Louis Kronenberger commented that "the melodrama itself constitutes a criticism of those who foment it. . . . They will stop at nothing—violence, knavery, treachery, all the forms of melodrama—to get what they want."[13] Jordan Miller concurs: "*The Little Foxes* is not melodrama as described by Owen Davis or as practiced by Augustin Daly, but it frequently employs melodrama with good effect."[14]

Viewing the 1967 revival, Walter Kerr wrote that Hellman lets the characters "treat the situation as simply something to be expected in a wryly wicked age. . . . Craft, and more than craft, is here at work. For the very plainness of the situation, the single-mindedness with which it is pursued, reflects a way of thinking, a habit of handling bonds and psyches as though they were equally negotiable, that did once exist . . . and may continue to characterize an age for some time to come" (*NYT*, Nov. 5, 1967).

And, finally, Henry Hewes, calling the Hubbards "the crass menagerie," said that "the play itself is demonstration, as it concentrates on showing us the graceless behavior of a society in which the more ambitious become scoundrels and the more decent stand by and let them get away with exploiting the poor." Hewes caught Hellman's ironic characterization of Ben, whose "ruthless exercise of power is frequently funny as it catches the irony that in this society undisguised malevolence can be more effective than guilt-weakened underhandedness" (*SR*, Nov. 11, 1967, p. 26).

(The Russians apparently saw a resemblance to Chekhov's *The Cherry Orchard*. A review of a 1946 production in Moscow tells us that "life stops for Birdie the day the trees on her beloved family estate are cut down.")[15]

Willard Thorp says in *American Writing in the Twentieth Century* that Hellman's "plots are carefully constructed but they are not 'well made' in the manner of Scribe and Sardou. . . . She is a specialist in the evil in men's lives, and as the titles of her plays suggest, she is also an ironist."[16] John Gassner, attempting to describe the tone of the play, uses the phrase "dark comedies": "The play exists, indeed, on many levels—as character drama, melodrama, and comedy. This is so decidedly the case that it is less easy than one would imagine to define the nature and ultimate effect of the play. . . . For an equivalent type of writing in the older drama one may have to go back to the 'dark comedies' of Shakespeare."[17]

One must remember that in Hellman's work "tone" is all-important; one must not let the play's "well-madeness" obscure the ironic approach, so much more obvious in *The Autumn Garden*, but certainly present in the earlier play.

Briefly, *The Little Foxes* is ironic in the way Birdie and Horace pass judgment on themselves, in the choral comments of Zan and Addie, and in the gathering of the clan for dinners and for Horace's homecoming. As in Chekhov's work, arrivals and departures bring about a change in the lives of the characters. *The Little Foxes* is also ironic in the revelation of the story in terms of a number of people, rather than a single protagonist. In fact, in no Hellman play is there a single protagonist; hence her titles are either thematic or symbolic references to a group of characters.

A reading of the criticism of *The Little Foxes* reveals that reviewers often think in terms of "good guys" and "bad guys," with the Hubbard crew as the villains ranged against Horace, Birdie, Alexandra, and Addie. One interesting audience response that critics have not commented on is the number of scenes involving only the Hubbards in which we root for one "little fox" against another. The plot conflict revolves not so much around whether the foxes will defeat the decent people but around who among the foxes will get the upper hand. From scene to scene, moment to moment, it is Oscar vs. Leo, Oscar-Leo vs. Ben, Ben vs. Regina, Ben-Regina vs. Oscar, Ben-Oscar vs. Regina. We enjoy—actually *enjoy* Ben and Regina's outwitting the duller Oscar, Ben's putting Leo in his place. We laugh *with* Ben and Regina and *at* Oscar and Leo. *We like their style*.

Ben and Regina differ from Oscar and Leo in more than intelligence. The former playact, are aware of each other's histrionics, even appreciate being bested by a better performance. And we laugh and applaud; we find them amusing, just as Lillian Hellman found her Uncle Jake amusing. Ben and Regina are performing for an audience—themselves—just as Uncle Jake was performing for his relatives at the family dinner described in *Pentimento*, in his response to a niece's questioning him about how poor people could use the toilets in his tenement building after he had removed the toilet seats and sold them: " 'Let us,' said Jake, 'approach your question in a practical manner. I ask you to accompany me now to the bathroom, where I will explode my bowels in the manner of the impoverished and you will see for yourself how it is done.' " The girl began to cry, whereupon her mother told her, " 'Go along immediately with your Uncle Jake. You are being disrespectful to him' " (p. 182). Hellman's Uncle Jake spoke the words Hellman gives to Regina at the end of the play, when she tells Zan she is glad to see that she isn't made of "sugar water."

In a notebook in which Hellman kept background notes, plot outlines, and tentative character descriptions, she describes Ben as "rather jolly and far less solemn than the others and far more dangerous" (*HT*, Sept. 24, 1939). Full of false joviality and platitudes which mask the shrewdness with which he operates, he blandly tells Zan goodbye before her trip to bring Horace home from Baltimore: "Have a nice trip, Alexandra. The food on the train is very good. The celery is so crisp. Have a good time and act like a little lady." The audience laughs at Ben's purring hypocritical geniality, knowing the bitter argument with Regina that preceded her decision to get Horace home. When Horace arrives unexpectedly in the middle of the Hubbards' breakfast, only Ben can mask his surprise and irritation at the late arrival. Deciding that it would be politic to leave the agitated Horace alone with Regina, Ben returns to his breakfast, saying, "Never leave a meal unfinished. There are too many poor people who need the food. Mighty glad to see you home, Horace. Fine to have you back. Fine to have you back."

Ben and Regina find each other amusing, even when one is being outwitted by the other. When Horace is late arriving from Baltimore, Regina tells Ben that he has probably stopped off to visit his cousin in Savannah. Ben points out that the cousin has been dead for some years and the train does not go through Savannah. Caught in a lie, Regina is amused and says in mock surprise to Ben, who laughs, "Did he die? You're always remembering about people dying. Now I intend to eat my breakfast in peace, and read my newspaper," and exits laughing.

Oscar often has to interpret Ben to the not-too-quick-witted Leo. In turn, Ben interprets their sister to Oscar, much to his own and Regina's amusement. When Regina insists on more than a third of the profits from the prospective cotton mill, slow-witted Oscar misunderstands her reasons. Ben straightens him out: "That isn't what Regina means. May I interpret you, Regina? (*To Oscar*) Regina is saying that Horace wants *more* than a third of our share.

Oscar: But he's only putting up a third of the money. You put up a third and you get a third. What else could he expect? Regina: Well, *I* don't know. I don't know about these things. It would seem that if you put up a third you should only get a third. But then again, there's no law about it, is there? I should think that if you knew your money was very badly needed, well, you just might say, I want more, I want a bigger share. You boys have done that. I've heard you say so." Regina and Ben smile and laugh throughout this exchange, which culminates with Oscar's asking, "And where would the larger share come from?" Regina answers, giggling, "I don't know. That's not my business. But perhaps it could come off your share, Oscar." Regina and Ben laugh. To placate Oscar, Ben asks Regina to consider marriage between Zan and Leo. Regina objects that they are cousins. Oscar says, "That isn't unusual. Our grandmother and grandfather were first cousins." Regina replies, "And look at us." She and Ben laugh. Oscar replies angrily, "You're both being very gay with my money."

One feels sure that, had the marriage actually been arranged and had Zan objected, someone would have said, "Do what your uncle says. You are being disrespectful to him."

Regina outwits her brothers, threatening them with exposure after Horace's death. When she says, "And as long as you boys both behave yourselves, I've forgotten that we ever even talked about [the stolen bonds]," Ben laughs, and Regina laughs with him. In another quick plot turn, when Alexandra implies that she is suspicious about her father's death, Ben says with a smile, "Alexandra, you're turning out to be a right interesting girl."

The ending of the play is ambiguous, an example of Hellman's "open-ended" technique. Some critics and reviewers dislike this construction. Richard Lockridge, reviewing the 1939 production, wrote, "Toward the end the movement falters and the pivotal character [Regina] . . . goes slightly out of focus" (*Sun*, Feb. 16, 1939). He is referring to the final scene between Alexandra and Regina: Regina tells Zan, "You're young, you shall have all the things I wanted. I'll make the world for you the way I wanted it to be for me. (*Uncomfortably*) Don't sit there staring. You've been around Birdie so much you're getting just like her." Zan tells her mother that she is going away from her because she wants to and because her father wanted her to. Regina replies, "Alexandra, I've come to the end of my rope. Somewhere there has to be what I want, too. Life goes too fast. Do what you want; think what you want; go where you want. I'd like to keep you with me, but I won't make you stay. Too many people used to make me do too many things. No, I won't make you stay." When Zan says that she is going somewhere where people don't stand around and watch other people eat the earth, Regina says, "Well, you have spirit, after all. I used to think you were all sugar water. We don't have to be bad friends. I don't want us to be bad friends, Alexandra. *(Starts, stops, turns to Alexandra)* Would you like to come and talk to me, Alexandra? Would you—would you like to sleep in my room tonight?" Alexandra, taking a step toward her, asks, "Are you afraid, Mama?" Without answering, Regina moves slowly out of sight, and the curtain falls.

Although Hollywood rewriting tends to make the endings of Hellman plays much more conclusive (one remembers Geraldine Page in *Toys in the Attic*, clinging to a wrought iron fence, begging her brother and sister not to leave her, and Karen and fiancé, in the remake of *The Children's Hour*, walking up the road from the cemetery while music swells around them), Hellman ends her plays on an indeterminate note, leaving us to wonder what the characters do with their lives. Even her war plays, *Watch on the Rhine* and *The Searching Wind*, with their upbeat endings, leave some questions unanswered.

In *The Little Foxes* Hellman bumps Regina slightly at the end, turning her just enough to show another facet of her character, as she moves slowly into the dark at the top of the stairs. Regina drops the playacting for an instant to show us another dimension. The "good guys" have speeches which are the equivalent of the Elizabethan "self-explaining monologue"; Oscar and Leo, on the other hand, are like "humor" characters. Even Ben never drops his mask. It is only Regina who hints that her life could have been different: "Oh, Ben, if Papa had only left me his money."

The characters in *The Little Foxes* are much more sharply differentiated by their speeches than are characters in *The Children's Hour* or *Days to Come*. Hellman accomplishes this difference with rhythm and idiom. Oscar's speech is jerky in rhythm, whiney in tone. Ben's is more expansive, more public in tone, as befitting a man who is always "on" for someone. Birdie, the lost alcoholic Southern lady, is more lyric and repetitive than the others: "I remember. It was my first big party, at Lionnet I mean, and I was so excited, and there I was with hiccoughs and Mama laughing. Mama always laughed. A big party, a lovely dress from

Mr. Worth in Paris, France, and hiccoughs. My brother pounding me on the back and Mama with the elderberry bottle, laughing at me. Everybody was on their way to come, and I was such a ninny, hiccoughing away. . . . Like I say, if we could only go back to Lionnet. Everybody'd be better there. They'd be good and kind. I like people to be kind. Don't you, Horace; don't you like people to be kind?"

Birdie's speeches are like arias. As she drinks wine and continues to reminisce in that leisurely scene with Horace, Addie, and Zan, the calm before the storm, she ceases to repeat herself as she realizes what has become of her life and warns Zan not to make the same mistake: "And that's the way you'll be. And you'll trail after them, just like me, hoping they won't be so mean that day or say something to make you feel so bad—only you'll be worse off because you haven't got my Mama to remember—"

But Birdie is not intended to be Blanche DuBois; Hellman is an ironist. Looking at *The Little Foxes* as the work of an ironist and using Robert Boies Sharpe's *Irony in the Drama* as a basis, we can find more than one kind of irony in *The Little Foxes*. Hellman raises the level of impersonation in the play by giving us characters (Ben and Regina) who assume roles when dealing with other people. They playact, as we have seen. Thus, above the level of the simple impersonation of the character by an actor, we have the character assuming a hypocritical role. We have another kind of irony in characters who have knowledge other characters lack and who consequently speak ironically. Regina explains Ben to Oscar; Ben explains Regina. They talk for his benefit. Or, as Sharpe puts it, we have "situations where one or more characters who are conscious of the ironies produce by ironic words and visible means a sense of cross-purposes."[18]

Enclosing these ironies is dramatic irony. The audience knows more than the characters. In *The Children's Hour* the defendants know the outcome of the trial before we do, and we learn at the same time Karen does that Mrs. Tilford wants to make amends. In *The Little Foxes*, however, we know before Ben and Oscar that Regina knows about the bonds; we know before Regina that Ben and Oscar don't need Horace's money, and we realize that Horace is charting his own doom when he repeatedly says that Regina won't have her way as long as he is alive.

The plot employs what Sharpe calls "boomerang irony." The stolen bonds which temporarily free Ben and Oscar from Regina put them in her control when Horace dies. And Regina, apparently freeing herself completely by allowing Horace to die, is left at the end with the threat of disclosure when Alexandra's question, "What was poppa doing on the stairs?" arouses Ben's suspicion. Even Horace's effort to outwit Regina boomerangs; his threat to make a new will leaving only the bonds to Regina causes his death.

The Little Foxes contains still another element which Sharpe considers important in ironic drama—the sense of false happiness and security before the catastrophe. Sharpe tells us to "look just before the turning points of the most powerful comedies. . . . Some of the clearest instances . . . occur in comedies of a satirical tinge which come rather close to tragedy" (p. 148). In *The Little Foxes* Hellman gives us Horace, Alexandra, Addie, and Birdie in a scene of momentary happiness planning for the future.

Permeating the other ironies is their source, Hellman's ironic view of the character and the situation, "a view of life, a mood, a psychological state (brief or sustained) which in the theater is communicated from playwright, by way of director and actor, to audience; and . . . the artistic means to the communication of that mood of irony, the techniques used by playwright, director, and actor to put the audience into that psychological state" (Sharpe, p. ix).

Kenneth Rowe says in *A Theater in Your Head* that the plays that interest us are those "in which there is life seen through a temperament, life interpreted or experienced in the light of a distinctive mind," adding "There is a fine distinction of mind in Lillian Hellman's plays, . . . a hard rationality and moral clarity, that is sometimes not fully recognized because of the very apparent workmanlike craftsmanship in conventional form and her exact rather than electrifying use of language of direct communication." [19]

Hellman sees the Hubbards as funny in their role-playing and scheming; funny, but dangerous. Set against them are not the pure and virtuous of the melodrama, but people who allowed them to rise. Addie is helpless because she is black; Zan has been helpless because she is young. But Birdie and Horace represent the people who allowed the Hubbards to take over. Horace worked for them and made money for them and for himself before his illness forced him into soul-searching. And Birdie—is she, as Hardwick said, an example of "besieged Agrarianism" whom we should shed tears for? On the contrary, Hellman's Birdie is a silly, lost, pathetic woman, representative of a class that learned nothing from the Civil War, that felt that being "good to their people" made them superior to William Faulkner's Snopeses and the Hubbards. (The Hubbards are Snopeses who have been rich long enough to acquire a thin middle-class veneer of respectability. Oscar worries about what people will think when Birdie runs across the Square in her robe.)

Like the Snopeses, the Hubbards are driven by a lust for power and money rather than by sex, a motivation to which we shall return. Like the Snopeses, the Hubbards turn on one another and find a certain wry-mouthed humor in the display of their own trickery.

Birdie, with her Wagner autograph (she refers to Wagner and his wife as she would her neighbors, as "Mr. and Mrs. Wagner") and her memories of gowns from "Paris, France" purchased at Worth's ("Mr. Worth," to Birdie—one gathers she would refer to the plays of "Mr. Shakespeare"), is given not as an alternative to the Hubbards, a specimen of "besieged Agrarianism," but as a contributing factor in their rise. Her "arias" in Act III are followed by Addie's words about the people who stand around and watch other people eat the earth. Addie is indeed talking to Birdie and Horace. Like Faulkner's Compsons and Sartorises, the gentry chose to lose themselves in nostalgia, dreams, and drink rather than build a better South, creating a vacuum which the Hubbards rushed to fill. (Hellman suggests that Regina and her brothers dealt rather directly with the attempt of Horace and Birdie to escape genteelly into music. We learn that Horace's bank box contains a piece of a broken violin—broken, no doubt, by Regina.)

Returning to the Hubbard motivation, one may feel that money rather than sex as a driving force is comic. In fact, envy and greed replace the desire for sexual satisfaction in Ben and Regina; and, as Jacob Adler points out, we find sex more interesting than money as character motivation, even though in "real life" it is probably money more often than sex that controls our destinies. As Chekhov wrote Suvorin, "Sex plays a great role in the world, but not everything depends on it and not everywhere is it of decisive importance." Men have died . . . and worms have eaten them, but not for love.

Envy and greed are antisocial vices and lend themselves to comic treatment. Obviously envy, along with greed, motivates the Hubbards. We learn that they have always been snubbed by "good families." It is true in the South to this day, in small towns at any rate, that descendants of "old families" are higher on the social ladder than "newcomers" who may have more money.

Regina is also envious of Ben and Oscar, who inherited their father's money. She envies Mrs. Marshall and the attractive ladies in Chicago, who do the things Regina wants to do. At least two critics have said that Hellman implies latent lesbianism in Regina. Their inference is based on Regina's denying Horace her bed and on her remark to Mr. Marshall about the ladies in Chicago—"I should like crowds of people, and theaters, and lovely women—*Very* lovely women, Mr. Marshall?"

Regina was forced to marry Horace because her father left all the money to the boys. She has as good a head for business as Ben, but in 1900 in Alabama there was no outlet for ambition in a woman except through her husband, who in Regina's case was not successful enough, did not have enough drive. Regina says to Birdie, "You know what I've always said when people told me we were rich? I said I think you should either be a nigger or a millionaire. In between, like us, what for?" Regina despises Horace for his weakness and for his "fancy women." Her remark to Marshall is not-very-subtle flirtatiousness. Regina is almost masculine in her drive for power. Before women's liberation, Regina would have been considered masculine; if anything, she is, like Lady MacBeth, unsexed.

Hellman's view of her characters as comic causes a distancing, a detachment on the part of the audience. Critic John Gassner is talking about *Another Part of the Forest* in the following remarks, but they apply equally well to *The Little Foxes*: "We can find that [European ironic] detachment virtually since *Commedia dell' arte*, if not earlier, and there are excellent examples of it since Machiavelli's *Mandragola* and the comedies of Molière to Becque's *The Vultures* and Carl Sternheim's plays. In the American drama, ironic detachment crops up rarely; it does in Lillian Hellman's plays and has been viewed with some misgivings, as may be seen from the New York reviewers' critical reaction to *Another Part of the Forest*." [20]

So we find a "dark comedy" of ironic detachment spoken of as melodrama, as a well-made play. Sharpe finds "the device of dramatic irony constantly being beaten down by the critics' confusing it with the artificial, lifeless trickeries of the well-made play" (p. 213). Assuming the play to be an expression of Hellman's private political views, critics have also considered it an attack on capitalism. When *The Little Foxes* was revived, the *Time* reviewer wrote that "its angle of vision is the leftism of the '30s. . . . A 1939 audience would have understood the play as an attack on predatory capitalist morality. A 1967 audience is more likely to relish it as an indictment of greed, hate, and the lust for power at any time, in any place" (Nov. 3, 1967, p. 69). A 1939 audience had the same reaction as the 1967 audience. Asked whether 1939 audiences laughed as much as audiences at the revival, Hellman said that in 1939 audiences laughed more because the revival lost some laughs through a piece of miscasting.

Hellman has always been sparing with stage directions. It might be well to add to the play some character descriptions like those of Tennessee Williams so that community theater directors, reading the original reviews, won't direct *The Little Foxes* as if it were *Seven Keys to Baldpate* or *Waiting for Lefty*, but will direct it as what it is—a dark, satiric comedy using melodramatic devices to make its point. As critic Malcolm Goldstein says, "A generation before the concept became modish, [Hellman] had devised a theater of cruelty and found an audience for it." [21]

CHAPTER 3

The Plays of the 1940s

I Watch on the Rhine

Lieb Vaterland, magst ruhig sein,
Fest steht und treu die Wacht am Rhein!
—German Patriotic Song

THE time is late in the spring of 1940. The place is a spacious home twenty miles from Washington, D.C., where dowager Fanny Farrelly lives with her bachelor son David. Refugee Roumanian Count Teck De Brancovis and his wife Marthe (daughter of a girlhood friend of Fanny's) are house guests. The count, a decadent aristocrat who has always lived by his wits, is a hanger-on at the German embassy. Fanny's daughter Sara arrives from Europe with her children and her husband Kurt Müller, a member of the underground resistance movement. Kurt is carrying $23,000 in a briefcase, money to be used to help rescue political prisoners from the Nazis.

The count discovers the money, figures out Kurt's identity, and tries to blackmail him by threatening to reveal that identity to the Germans. Kurt is forced to kill him, and Fanny and David, stripped of their American naiveté, decide to keep quiet about the murder long enough for Kurt to leave the country and return to Germany, where he will attempt to free the prisoners and will almost certainly be killed.

Kurt makes a moving farewell speech to his children in which he tells them that killing is always wrong and that he is fighting for a world where all men, women, and children can live in peace.

"There are plays that, whatever their worth, come along at the right time," says Hellman of *Watch on the Rhine* (*P*, p. 190). It was the right time—for Hellman, for the critics, and for the public. The

50

reviews were glowing, and President Roosevelt ordered a command performance at the National Theater in Washington.

Although many critics felt at the time that *Watch on the Rhine* was Hellman's best play, it has received little critical attention in subsequent years. In discussions of her work it is usually dismissed in a sentence or two as the best anti-Nazi play of the war years, although in 1941 it received the Drama Critics' award for the best play of the season. The Critics' award was presented for a "vital, eloquent and compassionate play about an American family suddenly awakened to the danger threatening their liberty." Herman Shumlin said he was not surprised that *Watch on the Rhine* won: "I have always thought from the day I read it that it was a great play and fine dramatic literature."

On opening night Shumlin stood in the lobby, hissing imprecations at people arriving late. Hellman had not been as sure of the play's success as Shumlin. Several reviewers commented on the bronchial opening night audience. Hellman sat through the first act, then went to Shumlin and told him, "It's no use, Herman. Make up your mind to it. This isn't going to go."

"Get out of here," Shumlin answered. "Get out and stay out. Don't you remember you said the same thing about *The Little Foxes*?" (*HT*, Apr. 9, 1944)

The command performance requested by Roosevelt was for the benefit of the Infantile Paralysis Fund. At a supper following the performance the President asked Hellman several times when she had written the play. Hellman says, "When I told him I started it a year and a half before the war, he shook his head and said in that case he didn't understand why Morris Ernst, the lawyer, had told him that I was so opposed to the war that I had paid for the 'Communist' war protesters who kept a continuous picket line around the White House before Germany attacked the Soviet Union. I said I didn't know Mr. Ernst's reasons for that nonsense story, but Ernst's family had been in business with my Alabama family long ago and that wasn't a good mark on any man."

She continues, "But the story about my connection with the picket line was there to stay, often repeated when the red-baiting days reached hurricane force. But by that time, some of the pleasant memories of *Watch on the Rhine* had also disappeared: Lukas, once so loud in gratitude for the play, put in his frightened, blunted knife for a newspaper interviewer" (*P*, p. 195).

But in 1941 there was mostly only praise for a fine, patriotic play. Except for Grenville Vernon's review, the strongest dissenting note came from the *New Masses* and the *Daily Worker*.

Authors of books about "radical theater" occasionally mention *Watch on the Rhine* as an example of a "leftist" play. The writer of such a work never deals with Hellman extensively, using such reasons as Hellman's not having written enough plays in the 1930s for adequate analysis, although three plays would seem to be ample. The writers then use Odets, Lawson, *et al.* A more likely reason for Hellman's exclusion from such treatments is that her plays do not fit the writers' theses. She wrote *The Little Foxes*, not "*Waiting for Horace.*" As Hellman told Roosevelt, she had been working on *Watch on the Rhine* since 1939, and the play opened while the Nazi-Soviet Non-Aggression pact was still in effect.

Aside from the anti-fascist content of the play, the character of Kurt Müller, the resistance fighter, received the most attention. Critics praised Hellman for making the protagonist, as they so regarded him, German. Müller is described by reviewers as the protagonist, the central figure, the principal character, "her hero." If one feels that there is a single protagonist, then other criticisms follow. George Freedley, for example, complained that Hellman had "cluttered her play with sub-plots and extraneous action to such an extent to obscure what might have been her best play" (*Morning-Telegraph*, Apr. 3, 1941).

Let us assume for the moment that *Watch on the Rhine* is not solely about Kurt Müller, but is also the story of Fanny Farrelly, a matriarch from another time (her husband knew Henry Adams, and in Adams's day Washington was a relatively small, sleepy Southern town); of her son David, who has never asserted himself, but who has allowed his mother to attempt to make him into his father's image (Joshua's portrait watches over the living room, and Fanny refers to him often); of Marthe, an American who was forced by her mother to marry a title; and of the Roumanian count, European like Kurt Müller, but of the type who let Hitler happen, whose only interest is self-aggrandizement and survival.

In other words, let us assume that *Watch on the Rhine* is like *Days to Come*, *The Little Foxes*, *The Searching Wind*, *Another Part of the Forest*, *The Autumn Garden*, and *Toys in the Attic*—a multiple-character play. What, then, is the play about? "What it contrasts are two ways of life—ours with its unawakened innocence and Europe's with its tragic necessities" (*Post*, Apr. 2, 1941). The contrast is presented in a sunny, spacious living room, a setting completely alien to the horrors occurring in Europe. But the watch on the Rhine comes to the Potomac, causing the Americans to be "shaken out of the magnolias." They learn what Alexandra learned in *The Little Foxes*, "that the fundamental clash in civilization is between those bent on self-aggrandizement and those who are not and that 'it doesn't pay in money to fight for that in which we believe' " (*NYT*, Aug. 28, 1943). There are those who eat the earth and those who stand around and watch them eat it.

We meet the Americans and their house guests at breakfast, and their characters are firmly established before the arrival of the Müllers. As Richard Watts said, Hellman provides the "comfortable feeling that the play you are watching is a living, breathing thing, with people in it who have a life of their own outside the narrow confines of the theater's walls, and thus are engaging in activities that have significance about them. All good plays obviously give some sense of this, but not all of them have the three-dimensional quality in so complete a fashion as 'Watch on the Rhine,' and for this I think the much-criticized first act . . . is in great part responsible" (*HT*, May 18, 1941).

The contrast, not only between Europeans and Americans but between two European-American marriages, may remind one of Henry James. (James Agee, reviewing the movie version, said he wished James had written it.) This resemblance is not coincidental, although Hellman says today that only diaries of the time "could convince [her] now that *Watch on the Rhine* came out of Henry James" (*P*, p. 185). At the time of the original production Hellman told an interviewer, "When I was working on 'The Little Foxes' I hit on the idea—well, there's a small, Midwestern American town, average or perhaps a little more isolated than average, and into that town Europe walks in the form of a titled couple—a pair of titled Europeans—pausing on their way to the West Coast. . . .

"Later I had another idea. What would be the reactions of some sensitive people who had spent much of their lives starving in Europe and found themselves as house guests in the home of some very wealthy Americans? What would they make out of all the furious rushing around, the sleeping tablets taken when there is no time to sleep them off, the wonderful dinners ordered and never eaten . . . ? . . . That play didn't work either. I kept worrying at it, and the earlier people, the titled couple, returned continually. It would take all afternoon and probably a lot of tomorrow to trail all the steps that made those two plays into 'Watch on the Rhine.' The titled couple are still in, but as minor characters. The Americans are nice people, and so on. It all is changed, but the new play grew out of the other two" (*NYT*, Apr. 20, 1941).

In *Pentimento* Hellman says that she dreamed one night of the poker party in London at which she met the man who suggested the Roumanian count in *Watch on the Rhine*. Wanting to "write a play about nice, liberal Americans whose lives would be shaken up by Europeans, by a world the new Fascists had won because the old values had long been dead," she used the setting of an Ohio town. Waking from the dream, she knew that she "had stubbornly returned to the people and the place of *Days to Come*." She changed the setting to Washington, introduced the character of Kurt Müller, who "was, of course, a form of Julia," Hellman's girlhood friend killed by the Nazis (*P*, pp. 186–87). (Hellman eventually used her notion about European reaction to affluent Americans in *The Autumn Garden*. The profession of Fanny Farrelly's husband, diplomacy, is used in *The Searching Wind*.) *Watch on the Rhine* is, in a sense, her tribute to Julia, and also to the men "willing to die for what they believed in" whom she had seen in the Spanish Civil War.

Perhaps Kurt Müller seems the lone protagonist not only because Hellman wrote the role with passion and admiration, but because he acts with decision and courage and is Hellman's most eloquent spokesman for human rights and liberty. But the other characters are faced with ethical choices because of his arrival. At the end of the first act Marthe warns Teck against harming Kurt. She tells him she will leave him if he makes trouble. At the end of the second act, Teck asks her to leave with him. She refuses, saying, "You won't believe it, because you can't believe anything that hasn't got tricks to it, but David hasn't much to do with this. I told you I would leave someday, and I remember where I said it—and why I said it."

Kurt tells Fanny and David that Teck has discovered the $23,000 Kurt is carrying, "gathered from the pennies of the poor who do not like Fascism." When Fanny asks whether it wasn't careless of him to "leave twenty-three thousand dollars lying around to be seen," Kurt answers, "No, it was not careless of me. . . . It was careless of you to have in your house a man who opens baggage and blackmails." David and Fanny take the first step toward joining Kurt's side when they offer to pay Teck themselves. But they still don't understand completely. David tells Kurt he will be safe: "You're in this country.

They can't do anything to you. They wouldn't be crazy enough to try
it. Is your passport all right?" When Kurt says it isn't quite, Fanny
asks why it isn't. Kurt says, "Because people like me are not given
visas with such ease. . . . Madame Fanny, you must come to
understand it is no longer the world you once knew."

Still failing to understand, David tells Kurt, "It doesn't matter.
You're a political refugee. We don't turn back people like you." Sara
says, "You don't understand, David," and explains that Kurt has to
go back to Germany.

In Act III Teck reads from a German embassy list of wanted men
a description of Kurt's underground activities. When Fanny says
she is sickened by Teck, Kurt makes a key speech: "Fanny and
David are Americans and they do not understand our world—as yet.
(*Turns to David and Fanny*) All Fascists are not of one mind, one
stripe. There are those who give the orders, those who carry out the
orders, those who watch the orders being carried out. Then there
are those who are half in, half hoping to come in. . . . Frequently
they come in high places and wish now only to survive. They came
late: some because they did not jump in time, some because they
were stupid, some because they were shocked at the crudity of the
German evil, and preferred their own evils, and some because they
were fastidious men. For those last, we may well someday have
pity. They are lost men, their spoils are small, their day is gone. (*To
Teck*) Yes?" And Teck replies, "Yes. You have the understanding
heart."

When Fanny and David leave the room to get the money, Teck
says, "The new world has left the room. . . . We are Europeans,
born to trouble and understanding it. . . . They are young. The
world has gone well for most of them. For us—we are like peasants
watching the big frost. Work, trouble, ruin—But no need to call
curses at the frost. There it is, it will be again, always—for us." Teck
is almost pitiable. Sara counters his effectiveness, however, by
speaking up and saying, "We know how many there are of you.
They don't, yet. My mother and brother feel shocked that you are in
their house. For us—we have seen you in so many houses."

After Kurt kills Teck, he says, "I have a great hate for the violent.
They are the sick of the world. Maybe I am sick now, too." A gentle
man, a man of peace, driven to murder to protect the cause he is
fighting for, he says to his children as he prepares to leave them,
"Do you remember when we read *Les Misérables*? . . . He stole
bread. The world is out of shape we said, when there are hungry

men. And until it gets in shape, men will steal and lie and—and—
kill. But for whatever reason it is done, and whoever does it—you
understand me—it is all bad. I want you to remember that.
Whoever does it, it is bad."

Fanny and David make their decision when Kurt tells them they
can either phone the police or wait two days to give him a head
start, making themselves, in effect, accessories to murder. Fanny,
agreeing to help him, makes another key speech. A critic once
complained that we know what Hellman is against, but we don't
know what she is *for*. Fanny's speech tells us. "I was thinking about
Joshua. I was thinking that a few months before he died, we were
sitting out there." She points to the terrace. "He said, 'Fanny, the
complete American is dying.' I said what do you mean, although I
knew what he meant, I always knew. 'A complete man,' he said, 'is a
man who wants to know. He wants to know how fast a bird can fly,
how thick is the crust of the earth, what made Iago evil, how to plow
a field. He knows there is no dignity to a mountain, if there is no
dignity to man. You can't put that in a man, but when it's there, put
your trust in him!' "

At the end of the play, left alone on stage with David, Fanny says,
"We are shaken out of the magnolias, eh?" David asks her if she
understands that they are going to be in for trouble. Fanny replies,
in a line reminiscent of *The Little Foxes* but spoken to a much
different purpose, "I understand it very well. We will manage. I'm
not put together with flour paste. And neither are you—I am happy
to learn."

Hellman is not an ironist in this play inasmuch as the tone of the
whole play is not ironic. Kurt and Sara are presented as admirable
characters; Fanny and David are likable, though naive, and rise to
the moral occasion. Marthe is treated sympathetically. Even Teck is
not presented with the ironic scorn one feels in *The Little Foxes*.

The title is ironic, coming from a German patriotic song, as the
Americans learn that they must keep watch on the Potomac. There
is ironic dialogue as Teck and Kurt talk over the heads of Fanny and
the children in the second act. Fanny makes humorously ironic
comments about other people, as does David.

We find an example of "boomerang irony" in Teck's blackmail
threat, which causes his death, and again Hellman employs
dramatic irony, letting the audience know Teck's plans, Kurt's work
as a member of the resistance movement, Fanny's misgivings about
David and Marthe. Again we have the tranquil moment before the
climax, as Act II opens ten days after the Müllers' arrival, with

Joshua playing baseball with Joseph, the butler; Babette sewing; and Bodo repairing the maid's heating pad, while Kurt plays the piano. Into this warm setting comes Teck, with his barbed remarks; and, as background to his probing questions, we hear the piano, played by a man with broken hands, broken by the Nazis.

Hellman's character development has been so thorough, almost novelistic, that we are prepared to accept Fanny's decision to help Kurt and David's love for Marthe. We have seen Fanny as the autocrat of the breakfast table, but we have also seen that, though a strong woman, given to raising her voice when she doesn't get her way, she is generous, loving, an old-fashioned liberal, of a day when the word meant something. And, before the climactic scene, David has been led to assert himself because of his love for Marthe.

We have seen, as so often we see in a Hellman play, the clash of generations. This time, the conflict is resolved. As Sara says, she comes of good stock, and both generations, shaken out of the magnolias, join to face the danger threatening their family and their country.

By the end of the play each character has committed a definitive act. In a strange essay, Elizabeth Hardwick says that "in most of [Hellman's] plays there are servants, attractive people, money, expensive settings, agreeable surroundings and situations for stars. It is typical of her practice that when she writes in *Watch on the Rhine* of a German refugee coming to America in 1940, he goes not to the Bronx or Queens or even to Fort Washington Avenue, but to a charming country house near Washington" (*NYRB*, Dec. 21, 1967).

In a delightful response, Richard Poirier pointed out that, if Hardwick had used her own definition of melodrama, "it might have kept her, too, from complaining that the German refugees in *Watch on the Rhine* did not go to Fort Washington Avenue instead of to a country house near Washington, D.C., where, freed of commuting, they could spend more time in the kind of environment to which Hellman wanted to expose them" (*NYRB*, Jan. 18, 1968).

Like Henry James, Hellman is a humanist, not a determinist; she believes in free will and personal responsibility for one's actions or failure to act. Hellman's concern with ethical choices has caused her to study the behavior of the well-to-do because their money gives them the freedom to make moral choices, to deal with moral responsibilities. To send the refugees to the Bronx would have destroyed the theme of the play.

In *Watch on the Rhine* we see a theme with which we are already familiar and which we shall see again in *The Searching Wind*; our world is the sum of our personal acts. Perhaps this concern with ethical responsibility led Bette Davis to accept the relatively minor role of Sara Müller in the screen version. Miss Davis said that she took the part because she believed *Watch on the Rhine* "had something important to say at a time when it could do the most good."[1]

The film script was included in John Gassner's *Best Film Plays of 1943–1944*, and the film itself was voted the best movie of the year by the New York film critics. The play was successful on tour, as were productions in Europe and London. It was done after the war in Moscow, and in Germany, where it was called *On the Other Side.*

How would the play fare today? How much of the critical fervor was caused by the topicality? How would it strike a "turned-off" generation? In the 1960s Edward Albee announced plans to produce the play, but it was never done. Perhaps Hellman felt that audiences might view *Watch on the Rhine* as support for the war in Vietnam, which she opposed. She said at the time of the Broadway production, "In 'Watch on the Rhine,' I find the play so variously interpreted on every hand that I have decided it is so fluid a script anybody can bring to it any meaning they want to" (*HT*, May 18, 1941).

Viewed solely as a melodrama, solely as the story of Kurt Müller, the play may be dated. But, if it is the story of some nice, naive, liberal Americans put to the test; if it is a character drama, like *The Autumn Garden*, then it still should have validity. Until, however, a revival allows us to judge for ourselves, we can view it as probably the best of the World War II anti-Nazi plays, or we can agree with Brooks Atkinson that "since Miss Hellman has communicated her thoughts dramatically in terms of articulate human beings, 'Watch on the Rhine' ought to be full of meaning a quarter of a century from now when people are beginning to wonder what life was like in America when the Nazi evil began to creep across the sea" (*NYT*, Aug. 24, 1941).

II The Searching Wind

The place is Washington, D.C.; the time, the spring of 1944. Diplomat Alexander Hazen and his wife Emily have dinner with an old friend, Catherine (Cassie) Bowman. Emily and Cassie haven't met in years, although Emily knows that Alexander and Cassie have seen each other at intervals. Also at the dinner are Emily's father Moses Taney, retired newspaper publisher, and the Hazens' son Samuel, who has been severely wounded in the war and in fact will tell them at the end of the evening that his leg is to be amputated. In flashbacks the three former friends relive significant moments in their lives together: Mussolini's take-over in Italy, the rise of the Nazis in Germany, negotiations in Paris just before World War II.

Cassie loved Alex but wouldn't marry him because they quarreled about his lack of political conviction. The two women, though girlhood friends, were rivals. Though Emily married Alex, he and Cassie have met secretly through the years. The Hazens' son Sam denounces them at the end of the evening, and of the play, for doing nothing to prevent the events that led to the Second World War. Shaken, they face the truth about themselves and their actions.

Critics greeted *The Searching Wind* with some reservations, but generally hailed it as the best drama of the season. It was the last Hellman play directed by Herman Shumlin. Hellman herself directed her next play because, she told an interviewer, she was just tired of arguing.

Many comments on Hellman's work, written years after the productions, attribute political intentions to the writer; but *The Searching Wind* is the first Hellman play reviewed at the time as an expression of her political views. Some of the pieces (particularly George Jean Nathan's review) seem to review her alleged politics rather than the play itself. *The Searching Wind* nevertheless received seven votes from the Critics' Circle as the best play of the year, but was one short of a majority, and no award was given. Four of the Circle's members voted against any award, arguing that no American play was good enough that year.

The Searching Wind is an intelligently written play. In a sense, it is an extension of *Watch on the Rhine*—Joshua Farrelly was a diplomat; in an early draft of the latter play David had a wife, Emily, who was jealous. Emily is the name of the wife in *The Searching Wind*. The character of Moses, the grandfather in *The Searching Wind*, is much like that of Joshua Farrelly as described by his widow in *Watch on the Rhine*; and, like Joshua, Moses is a biblical name.

Hellman used some names of friends and family in *The Searching Wind*. Bowman is a family name, as we learn in *Pentimento*. Samuel is Dashiell Hammett's first name. And, not for the last time, we find a character named Sophronia.

Like *Watch on the Rhine*, *The Searching Wind* is contemporary;

in fact, the time in the opening scene is the spring of 1944, the time
of the production. The actual time span covered, however, is
twenty-two years. (Hellman originally conceived the play as
involving minor participants at the Versailles Peace Conference.)
Hellman uses flashbacks to show us how the middle-aged characters
arrived at their present plight and how their personal lives reflect
and influence the world they live in. In this sense the play is
reminiscent of *Days to Come*, making the point that the world is the
sum total of each person's personal actions.

There is no true villain in *The Searching Wind*. All of the major
characters have let things happen, have stood around and watched
the earth and the people on it be eaten. Nor is there a single
protagonist. A searching wind blows away the rationalizations of all
the characters by the end of the play, as they learn the truth about
themselves.

In the flashbacks we see the characters at crucial moments in the
history of their lives and in the history of the western world.
Perhaps the attempt to tell two stories at once makes the impact of
the play diffuse, although the theme is clear enough. At turning
points in the history of Western Europe between two world wars,
the principal characters, with the exception of Cassie, failed to take
a moral stand. And Cassie, by quarreling with Alexander Hazen,
lost the opportunity to influence his diplomatic decisions.

The characterization of Cassie may have frustrated the reviewers.
She appears to be Hellman's spokesman: in a Hellman play a
character illustrating Hellman's viewpoint often has a confrontation
scene with other characters. In *The Searching Wind* these scenes
occur offstage, with the exception of Cassie's last speech to Alex and
Emily. Because Cassie has more life, is more assertive than Emily
and Alexander, we are interested in what happens to her. But we
never see her alone with Alexander except in a brief scene in Paris
just before Chamberlain goes to Munich.

The quarrel that ends the engagement occurs offstage. We are
told about it, offhandedly, in the scene in the German restaurant.
Cassie asks, "What did Alex tell you when he came back from seeing
me? When he came back to Rome where you were waiting for him?"
Emily replies, "I didn't make you and Alex fight. I didn't even know
you'd had a fight for months after he came back to Rome. Then all
he ever told me was that you disagreed with what he thought and
what he was, and that you'd both decided to quit. What good is this,
Cassie? It's all over, now." (Act II, Scene 1)

We are told again and again that Alex and Cassie meet, but we never see the meetings. How did Alex propose to Emily? Was it then that he told her about Cassie? We don't know. What do Alex and Cassie talk about in their meetings? When we see Cassie, she is Alex's "intellectual conscience." Do they argue when they meet alone?

The flaw in the play, then, is that it is Cassie who interests us, and her story is not told. Hers is the most forceful dialogue. In Rome she says to Alex, "A revolution is going on out there. But by this time next year it will be nothing more than dinner-table conversation. Things mean so little to us, to you—" And to Emily, "Do stop playing the piano. It doesn't go well with guns." When they meet in Berlin, in the middle of a Jewish pogrom, Alex says, "I want to go to the police. We'll make a strong official protest. Put it on the grounds that many Americans are in Berlin—" Cassie says, "Couldn't you put it on the grounds that it's a horror and a disgrace? Or would that be too simple?" In Paris, Alex tells Cassie that he doesn't know what's best. She says, "Back doing business at the old stand, Alex?"

It is Cassie who at the end of the play explains to herself and the others what they have done with their lives. Her final big speech is clear, emphatic, almost impassioned. The play would have been strengthened if it had ended with Cassie's speech, with responses from Emily and Alex. Sam's curtain speech is superfluous.

Hellman obviously intended Sam to show us that the sins of the fathers (and grandfathers) are visited on the children. But the same purpose would have been served if news of Sam's death in battle had been received in the last act. The problem with the character of Samuel is that we are told throughout the play that he exists, but we never feel about him, as we do about so many Hellman characters, that he had a life prior to 1944. He is not developed adequately. He appears to exist only to make Hellman's point about one generation's being affected by another's errors and to make the curtain speech.

Flawed though it is, *The Searching Wind* is similar to other Hellman plays in many ways. Its title is symbolic. Hellman told an interviewer that she got the title from a Negro maid: "Some mornings when she came she'd say 'It's a searching wind today.' She meant one of those winds that go right through you to your backbone. I suppose in my title I was thinking of the wind that's blowing through the world" (*HT*, Apr. 9, 1944). She also told Ward Morehouse, however, that she got the title from Dickens's novel *Bleak House* (*Sun*, Apr. 8, 1944).

In addition to the symbolic title, Hellman uses the irony of

repetition and "boomerang irony." Alexander went to World War I
because no one acted to prevent that war. He feels that his father's
description of France didn't match what he saw at first hand. Sam
feels that the Italy he fought in doesn't fit the Italy Alexander
describes; and Sam goes to war, of course, because his father's
generation let it happen. Cassie, by quarreling with Alex, loses the
chance to influence him to take a definite moral stand. Emily, who
influenced Alex to support appeasement because she didn't want
Sam to go to war, is then indirectly the cause of his being wounded.
Like the dowager in *Watch on the Rhine* and the matriarch to come
in *The Autumn Garden*, Moses makes ironic comments throughout
the play, but he is as guilty as the rest, having abdicated a position of
power and responsibility from which his viewpoint might have had
some influence.

Again Hellman employs dramatic irony, but not as thoroughly as
in earlier plays. We know before the characters do that Sam must
lose his leg. We know before Emily that Alex and Cassie have slept
together. But, since the organization of the play is basically that of a
"whodunnit," we learn much of the information along with the
characters. And some of what we are told we would rather see.
Strangely, Emily, the "detective" who instigates the search for the
truth in their lives, never explains why she wants to know in 1944
what she hadn't faced in twenty years. Alex tells Emily that she
hasn't wanted to see Cassie, nor has Cassie wanted to see her, and
asks, with us, why tonight? Cassie asks her, "Why did you ask me
here, why did I come? It's too difficult for us to meet again. Why did
you ask me, why did I come?—" Emily answers, "Because we
wanted to see each other again." Cassie says, "I don't think that's
the truth." Emily says she doesn't think so, either. The best
explanation we get is Emily's lines to Alex: "But there's a great deal
that you don't know, and Cassie doesn't know, and I don't, either.
It's time to find out." To which Cassie replies in a speech that might
fit in *The Autumn Garden*: "Leave it alone, Em. Leave it alone. It's
no good for people to sit in a room and talk about what they were, or
what they wanted, or what they might have been—" Motivation,
usually so crystal-clear in Hellman's work, is lacking. Emily remains
a rather cryptic figure.

If, as critics seemed to feel, *The Searching Wind* has plot
problems and deficiencies in characterization, what saved the play?
The answer is the dialogue—crisp, clear, often witty, and always
intelligent. Hellman had then and has now the finest mind of any

American playwright, and it is at work in this play in strong and incisive speeches. Emily says to Alex, "I don't mean to influence you with my money. I have it, I'm glad to have it, and it's never meant much to me. But I'm not willing to lie to myself about it, or where and how I was born, or the world I've lived in. But sometimes I think you pretend to yourself that you have no world that influences you—that you have no connections and no prejudices." And again to Alex: "If it makes you feel better to make fun of those people, then do it. But don't tell yourself that having contempt for them puts you on the opposite side." Moses says to Alex, who has made excuses for accepting appeasement, for compromising: "I feel sorry for people who are as tolerant as you," and "There's nothing like a good compromise to cost a few million men their lives."

In the definitive edition of her plays Hellman has cut some of the tense last scene, but leaves Cassie's big speech virtually intact. This speech is similar to closing speeches in *The Autumn Garden*, to Carrie's speech in *Toys in the Attic* about admitting what we know, and to Julie's speech in *Days to Come*. Cassie says,

> You know, when you don't think you're bad, then you have a hard time seeing you did things for a bad reason, and you fool yourself that way. It gets all mixed up and—maybe the hardest thing in the world is to see yourself straight. The truth is, I was haunted by Emily, all my life. You always said I talked too much about Emily and asked too many questions. I was angry when Emily married you—I felt it had been done against me. I had no plans then to do anything about it but—I wanted to take you away from Emily; there it is. It sounds as if I didn't care about you, but I did and I do. But I would never have done anything about you if I hadn't wanted, for so many years, to punish Emily—That's a lie. I did know it. I—This got in the way of everything: my work, other people. Well, I guess you pay for small purposes, and for bitterness. I can't say I'm sorry. I can say I got mixed up and couldn't help myself. I've always envied you, Emily. But if I learned about myself tonight, I also learned about you. And you, Alex. It's too bad that all these years I saw us wrong—Oh, I don't want to see another generation of people like us who didn't know what they were doing or why they did it. You know something? We were frivolous people. All three of us, and all those like us—Good-bye, my dear. (Act II, Scene 3, p. 320)

She moves to Emily, saying, "Somebody told me once that when something's been wrong with you and it gets cured, you miss it very much, at first. I'm going to miss you, in a funny kind of way." That is a powerful speech; the stage directions indicate that Cassie says the last part, about not wanting to see another generation of people like them, with great feeling. The play could, perhaps should, have ended with Alex's "Em, unless you want to, I'd like not to talk about it for a long time and then we can if—" Emily interrupts with "I don't ever want to talk about it. We'll just see how it works out." *The Autumn Garden* ends on just such a quiet note. The coda with Sam's speeches piles Pelion upon Ossa. It is not *The Children's Hour* or *Watch on the Rhine* that goes on too long—it is *The Searching Wind.*

Very little has been written about *The Searching Wind* in the years since the Broadway production. In 1945, Earl E. Fleischman (stage name, Eugene Earl), who had the minor role of Hazen's secretary in Paris, discussed the rehearsals of the play. He said that the play suffered in part from the playing and that part of that difficulty "could be laid at the door of the director. . . . The personal, emotional scenes tended to become stiff and mechanical, the pauses too long and deliberate, the intonation and emphasis too consciously rational." [2]

The only article after the initial reviews to deal with the play at length is Barrett H. Clark's in *College English* (December, 1944), which argues that "the theme in *The Searching Wind* is neither so obvious nor so clearly stated as it was in *Watch on the Rhine*, because by its very nature it is hardly susceptible of perfect definition." He quotes Moses' speech in Rome, " 'I knew most of this years ago. But I should have known before that, and I did. But I didn't know I did. All night long I've been trying to find out when I should have known' " and asks, "How many of us knew what was happening, and what prevented our killing the evil before it took root and spread?" Clark goes on to say that Hellman set herself a difficult technical task in attempting to entwine the personal and the world situations, that she couldn't have used a *raisonneur* without spoiling the surface realism and concludes:

That *The Searching Wind* is neither so appealing nor so wholly satisfactory as *The Little Foxes* or *Watch on the Rhine*, . . . its means of achieving revelation are somewhat awkward, and . . . its implications are not entirely convincing—this is not very important: the play relies to a remarkable extent on the characterization and not on the story, on the dialogue and not on the plot; it needs no violence other than the violence precipitated by the impact of person on person, idea upon idea. Most notable, however, is the author's own attitude toward the problem she wants to set forth. She is no longer the special pleader for this or that type of reform, and she is evidently not ridden by the notion that all you have to do to win the Good Life is to eradicate the evil men and substitute the good (pp. 132–133).

How did Hellman feel about her play in the forties and how does she feel today? In 1944 she told an interviewer that *The Searching Wind* pointed out that "there were not only a lot of bastards who fixed things up in the last 10 or 12 years, but nice people, too, who can do bad things from the right motives." Asked whether she started with a message, she said emphatically that message writing "makes the worst kind of writing" and added, "I know I *don't* start by telling myself to write a play about War. What war. Whose war? What occurs to me first are the people" (*PM*, Mar. 12, 1944).

She told a *New York Times* interviewer, "I don't believe in so-called thematic writing. You know the people in the play and those people have to say and do what they have to say and do. Not even 'Watch on the Rhine' was thematic" (*NYT*, Oct. 23, 1949). Twenty years later, she said, "I've never been interested in political messages, so it is hard for me to believe I wrote them. Like every other writer, I use myself and the time I live in. The nearest thing to a political play was *The Searching Wind*, which is probably why I don't like it much any more. But even there I meant only to write about nice, well-born people who, with good intentions, helped to sell out a world." Asked whether she was more concerned with the situation than with the characters, she said, "Yes. But I didn't know that when I was writing it. I felt very strongly that people had gotten us into a bad situation—gotten us into a war that could have been avoided if fascism had been recognized early enough" (*WW*, p. 132).

III   Another Part of the Forest

The place is Bowden, Alabama; the time, June 1880. Marcus Hubbard, father of Ben, Oscar, and Regina of *The Little Foxes* fame, is a self-made man who got his start smuggling during the Civil War. During the war he inadvertently led Union troops to an encampment of local boys, who were killed. Only his semi-mad wife Lavinia knows his secret. He dotes on Regina and torments his sons.

Regina is in love with John Bagtry, ex-Confederate officer and plantation owner, who wants only to go to Brazil to fight again. Regina wants to marry him and go to Chicago. His cousin Birdie

comes to Ben to borrow money to keep the family plantation going.
Increasing the amount, Ben proposes the loan to his father as a good
business investment, planning to pocket the difference. Oscar wants
enough money to go to New Orleans with the local whore, whom he
"deeply and sincerely" loves.

Ben invites Birdie and John Bagtry to his father's "musicale" and
has Oscar invite his love Laurette. Ben hopes to thwart Regina's
plan and get his father enraged at Oscar. He tells Marcus about
Regina's desire to marry Bagtry. In return Regina exposes Ben's
finagling. Marcus orders Ben to leave. As Ben tells his mother
goodbye, she babbles as she has throughout the play that she wants
to go away and start a school for black children. She reveals she
knows a secret dangerous to Marcus. Ben coaxes it from her by
promising to give her the money for the school and confronts his
father with his knowledge, threatening to tell the townspeople the
truth. As the curtain comes down, Oscar has lost his deep-and-
sincere love, Regina has lost Bagtry and Chicago, and Ben is in
command, a position acknowledged by Regina, who moves from her
habitual place by Marcus at the breakfast table to sit by Ben.

Another Part of the Forest evoked some of the same kind of
confusing criticism given *The Little Foxes*. Hellman says in
Pentimento that "in 1946 it seemed right to go back to [the
Hubbards'] youth, their father and mother, to the period of the
Civil War. I believed that I could now make clear that I had meant
the first play as a kind of satire. I tried to do that in *Another Part of
the Forest*, but what I thought funny or outrageous the critics
thought straight stuff; what I thought was bite they thought sad,
touching, or plotty and melodramatic. Perhaps, as one critic said, I
blow a stage to pieces without knowing it" (p.197).

As with *The Little Foxes*, no one quite understood *Another Part
of the Forest*. A typical review tells us, "One leaves the theatre
exhausted, so intense has been the portrayal of family intrigue,
jealousy, contempt, and revenge. It is morbid, horrible in the
intimacy of its 36 hours of crisis, in the exchange of power in the
household, in the diabolical play upon old fears and control of an
insane mind" (*Wilmington News*, Nov. 2, 1946). "Morbid," "horrible," and "diabolical" hardly seem the words to describe a play that
is as funny as *The Little Foxes*, but broader, as if Hellman had
attempted to spell things out for people who had misunderstood the
earlier play. The critics just didn't quite get her satirical intentions,
however. Since "everyone knew" that Hellman was a social critic

and a writer of melodrama, then *Another Part of the Forest* had to be, perforce, a melodramatic study of the rise of capitalism.

A few reviewers did mention that they found the play funny; others, however, thought the humor unintentional, a result of melodrama's being carried too far. They used words like "burlesque" and "travesty," but assumed that a dead-serious Hellman, pen dipped in red, had overdrawn pictures of capitalists like political cartoonist Thomas Nast. Other critics assumed she had tried to write a tragedy and fallen short, into melodrama.

Hellman said at the time that she had "tried to say pretty much what 'The Little Foxes' said. This is the beginning. The time is 1880. The play starts on a Sunday and is over Tuesday morning. This is an absolutely separate play. It's not necessary to have seen the 'Foxes.' There is never a reference to it. I was careful about that. The characters have the same names but it's really a new play and really new people" (*Sun*, Nov. 15, 1946).

Although the play can stand alone, Hellman made the characterizations generally consistent with those of *The Little Foxes*; yet there are some discrepancies. Birdie's brothers were killed in the war and consequently didn't live to ruin Lionnet. Birdie is too young to have witnessed the parties she remembers in *The Little Foxes*. These small items, however, are no more important than the minor inconsistencies one finds in Faulkner's Yoknapatawpha saga. The characterizations superbly foreshadow the figures of *The Little Foxes* (although "foreshadow" may seem to be the wrong word to use about a "sequel-in-reverse," as critics called the play).

As John Gassner has pointed out more than once, Hellman writes dark comedies. Both *The Little Foxes* and *Another Part of the Forest* are in the tradition of *Volpone* and *Mandragola*. With the theory that the characters in *Another Part of the Forest* are obsessed, each with a fixed idea, let us examine the latter play.

The play opens on the porch of the Greek-revival house, where the last scene also takes place. Instead of our meeting the characters virtually en masse, as we do in *The Little Foxes*, we meet them singly. First, Regina in her "wrapper" hails John Bagtry, Birdie's cousin. The Civil War has been over fifteen years, but John wears part of a Confederate uniform. With only the one desire—to go to Brazil—Bagtry is a "burnt-out case," something like Chekhov's Ivanov in his relation to the young and vital Regina.[3]

When Ben enters, we witness the same battle of wits that he and Regina carried on in *The Little Foxes*. Hellman again depicts Ben as a role-player, literally a hypocrite; but Regina is different. She assumes a mask with Marcus, whose affection for her borders on the incestuous; but with Ben, she is fairly straightforward. If she appears more pliable with Bagtry than she really is, she is no more so than many young girls are to please their men. We early learn that Regina's twofold obsession is to marry John Bagtry and to go to Chicago.

Oscar is as simple-minded as he is in *The Little Foxes*, and his catch-phrase explains his obsession: he is "deeply and sincerely in love" with the town whore and wants to marry her and take her to New Orleans. He reminds us of his son Leo in *The Little Foxes* when he emerges onto the porch stuffing a biscuit in his mouth.

Lavinia, the foxes' dam, is unlike her children, who obviously take after their father. The traits that are not genetic have been formed by his strange and autocratic treatment of them. Lavinia, though broken and half-crazed from living with a man who shows only contempt for her, is a good woman, deeply religious in a childlike sense. She, too, has a specific obsession: to found a school for black children. (In creating Lavinia, Hellman may have used something of her mother's vague but sincere religiosity as described in *An Unfinished Woman* and *Pentimento*.)

Ben is the most interesting of the Hubbard progeny. In *Another Part of the Forest* Regina is no match for him because she still wants something human—love. Ben is already the Ben of *The Little Foxes*. He is interested only in money and the power it brings, and he has every reason to hate his father. When he gains the upper hand, he says to Marcus, "Don't waste your time, or put yourself in further danger, or tempt me longer. Ever since you started your peculiar way of treating me, many years ago, I have had ugly dreams. . . . You're a lucky man: you'll die in bed." (Act III) We can guess that the strange treatment started after Regina was born, fifteen years after Ben. Disappointed in his sons, Marcus placed in Regina his hopes for someone to share his love for culture.

With no concrete passions to cloud his judgment, Ben watches and waits for the others to make mistakes. When they do, he pounces. He can even be sardonic about being unloved. At the end of the play Ben asks his mother, "Do you like me, Mama?" Lavinia, after a pause, answers with, "Well. You've grown away from—I loved you, Benjamin." Ben says, really to himself, "Once upon a time."

Since the reviewers apparently didn't see Birdie in *The Little*

Foxes as Hellman had intended them to, she added John Bagtry in the new play and gave Marcus a speech to spell out the meaning: John Bagtry says he thought the South would win. Marcus says, "I never did. Never, from the first foolish talk to the last foolish day," and then, "Your people deserved to lose their war and their world. It was a backward world, getting in the way of history. Appalling that you still don't realize it."

In Marcus, Hellman created what many critics regarded as her most interesting character. The prototype of all the iron-willed tyrants in Tennessee Williams, Marcus is more complicated. He despises his sons, and his feeling for Regina is his downfall.

What had been Marcus Hubbard's dream? Like Faulkner's Thomas Sutpen, Marcus Hubbard wanted to found a dynasty. One is reminded of Hellman's remark to Sam Goldwyn: "The trouble with you, Sam, is that you think you're a country." Marcus in a self-revealing soliloquy says, "At nine years old I was carrying water for two bits a week. I took the first dollar I ever had and went to the paying library to buy a card. When I was twelve I was working out in the fields, and that same year I taught myself Latin and French. At fourteen I was driving mules all day and most of the night, and that was the year I learned my Greek, read my classics, taught myself—Think what I must have wanted for sons. And then think what I got. One trickster, one illiterate." (Act II)

The outcome of his dream is in itself an irony.

The title of the play, as is usual with Hellman, is ironic. Hellman says she took it from a stage direction in Shakespeare's *As You Like It*. The meaning seems clear—in another stage action we are given the little foxes somewhere else, somewhen else.

In an ingenious explanation Manfred Triesch argues that the title and the characters of Marcus and Lavinia come from *Titus Andronicus* and finds a resemblance in the two Lavinias;[4] but since Hellman and her long-time press agent, Richard Maney, attribute the title to a stage direction in *As You Like It*, we should assume that is the source.

We again find characters who operate on more than one level of impersonation. Both Marcus and Ben speak sardonically and ironically to people who, most of the time, are incapable of understanding the hidden meaning. Ben, for example, doesn't want Birdie to talk to Marcus about the loan. When Birdie says she would never talk business at a party, Ben replies sardonically, "Good breeding is very useful." Regina occasionally speaks ironically, but, unlike the Regina of *The Little Foxes*, she can be open, as when she says to Ben, "Ben, don't. I'm in love with John."

Hellman employs dramatic irony throughout the play. We know what Regina's real plans are. We know the real deal Ben has made with Birdie. We know that Lavinia has the evidence to hang Marcus. We know before Regina and Oscar that their plans will be thwarted.

The structure of the play is "boomerang irony." "The gods are just, and of our pleasant vices/Make instruments to plague us." (*King Lear*, Act V, Scene 3) Had Marcus granted Lavinia's request, she would not have been present to be the instrument of his downfall. Had Marcus let Ben have the money to invest in coal, Ben would not have schemed to get it through Birdie, would not have been thwarted by Regina's trying to keep Bagtry from going to Brazil, would not have been ordered out of the house, and would not have gotten the information that gives him the upper hand. Regina's attempt to outwit Ben and keep Bagtry leads to her losing both Bagtry and Chicago and any freedom she had through her father's favoritism. Had Ben not defeated Marcus, Oscar would have been on his way to New Orleans with his deeply-and-sincerely-loved whore.

Like *The Little Foxes*, *Another Part of the Forest* shows us that the more intelligent Hubbards are good losers. When Oscar returns from the train, Marcus, Regina, and Ben join in mockery at Oscar's expense: Oscar tells them that Laurette left without him and, when he tried to carry her off the train, she spit at him: Regina says, "Spat in your face! How could she do a thing like that?" Marcus asks curiously, "How does one spit in your face?" Ben answers, "Why, I imagine the way one spits in anybody's face." Regina says, "But it's special in a railroad station. How did she do it, Oscar? You can't just up and spit—" Oscar, not realizing what the others are doing, says, spitting on the porch, "Just like that. The way you wouldn't do with a dog." Marcus, Regina, and Ben burst out laughing. Oscar, true to his "humor" character, soon lets his stomach distract his heart and is inquiring about breakfast.

Most reviewers still misunderstood Hellman's purpose and tone. Louis Kronenberger, for example, wrote, "Of all this Miss Hellman makes driving theater, and something more than driving theater—something more purposeful, more provocative, more talented. It is just because the play reaches higher ground that one wonders why it does not have quite the stature it should have. The answer, possibly, is that Miss Hellman's fable is not adequate to the force behind it. You cannot write off *Another Part of the Forest* as simply melodrama, for it is the people in the play that stay with us, not the plot. They are vigorous people, and Marcus is perhaps the most interesting character Miss Hellman has ever drawn. Yet to some extent melodrama has been permitted the last word" (*PM*, Nov. 22, 1946).

George Jean Nathan thought that Hellman had tried a "drama of hate and avarice in the Strindberg manner" and had wound up with "overwrought melodrama" which "so supervises character that the whole thing occasionally edges uncomfortably close to travesty" (*JA*, Dec. 2, 1946). Bentley said that "at some of the most hideous moments in Miss Hellman's play the audience laughs and is not altogether wrong in doing so. Like *The Little Foxes*, *Another Part of the Forest* is Grand Guignol in the guise of realism." [5] Kronenberger said that the play had "more than a little in common with those sombre Elizabethan 'comedies' swarming with cheats and knaves and evildoers." The *Cue* reviewer came closer to understanding the play than anyone else. He spoke of "continual overtones of humor," "sardonic chuckles at human error," and called it an "amusing study." He said that the characters were "not always above laughing at their own wickedness; and this, at times, gives them a peculiar quality almost approaching charm" (Nov. 30, 1946). John Gassner was right: "In the American drama, ironic detachment crops up rarely; it does in Lillian Hellman's plays and has been viewed with some misgivings, as may be seen from the New York reviewers' critical reaction to *Another Part of the Forest*." [6] Like *The Little Foxes, Another Part of the Forest*, from its title to its curtain, is not a melodrama. It is not a tragedy, failed or otherwise. It is an ironic, detached comedy.

Thirty years have passed since the Broadway production. If the play is revived, perhaps today we would at least be spared the Marxian label with which in 1946, as we moved toward the McCarthy era, someone always sought to tag Hellman. Joseph Wood Krutch said, "I am not unaware of the fact that all this is supposed to have, for the initiated, a meaning. It is, that is to say, a Marxian study." He saw the play as chronicling the "decline of the Southern feudal aristocracy and the rise of the capitalist exploiter. There are no admirable characters because, by antecedent premise, there cannot be any. Dying aristocrats must be dim-witted and rising capitalists must be villainous because otherwise the dialectic process could not have taken place as it did" (*Nation*, Dec. 7, 1946, p. 171). He does add that none of this is pointed out explicitly in the play.

Perhaps the most peculiar comment on the play was John Crosby's. Crosby, reviewing a Lux Radio Theater condensed version of *Another Part of the Forest*, starring Walter Huston as Marcus, Vincent Price as Ben, and Anne Blyth as Regina, described the play as being "as remorseless as the Comintern, with which Miss Hellman is sometimes accused of flirting." He described Hellman's major characters as "possessed of a single idea . . . and not to be deflected from it by any consideration at all. . . . Her characters are to my mind totalitarian individuals. . . . Miss Hellman professes to loathe totalitarianism . . . , but she nevertheless understands the totalitarian individual better than she understands the human or malleable individual. . . . She comprehends—I won't go so far as to say she sympathizes with—the undeviating man, as opposed to the rational man, and since the world seems now to be divided into two camps, . . . Miss Hellman, whom I consider the first literate exponent of the future totalitarian man, occupies a position of distinctive though unenviable importance in contemporary letters" (*HT*, Sept. 21, 1948).

The Politburo evidently lacked Mr. Crosby's insight into Hellman's work. *Another Part of the Forest* was performed in Moscow under the title *Ladies and Gentlemen* and, though popular with the audience, which sat through a five-hour performance and gave twelve curtain calls, the play aroused the ire of the official critics. A writer for *Soviet Art* criticized Hellman for not presenting a "merciless and scornful exposé of the awful capitalist reality." The article continued, "According to the idea of the author and producers of the play, in the Southern states there lived apparently only honest people who hate speculators and traitors. All of this is shown in the play, which claims to expose the ruling circles of the United States, in the days when there is unleashed reaction in threatening to lynch one of the most advanced people of America, Paul Robeson" (*NYT*, Nov. 13, 1949). It is little wonder that Hellman abandoned her original idea of writing a trilogy about the Hubbards, if critics found her "totalitarian" on one hand and failing to defend Paul Robeson on the other. As John Steinbeck observes in *A Russian Journal* (1948), one can't hope to satisfy "the lumpen right" and "the ecclesiastical left." As Lavinia says in the play, "People always believe what they want to believe."

Sydney J. Harris, writing for a Chicago paper, found a resemblance to Chekhov: "There is very little story in this story; nothing much 'happens' on the stage; most of the action is internal. But Miss Hellman's prose is so explosive and exploratory that she can generate drama in a phrase where it takes other playwrights a machine gun and four bodies crumpling to the floor." What Harris recognized was the ironic technique. The action in *Another Part of the Forest* centers around social groupings, breakfasts on the porch, and a "musicale" for which Marc Blitzstein composed the music. The musicale is a brilliant example of ironic demonstration. While Marcus's paid lackeys play his derivative pseudoclassical music in the background, the fate of each character is set by "boomerang irony." Ben's impending departure triggers the denouement. The characters make "self-explaining" speeches. We have already seen Marcus's explanation of himself. Ben says, "I spent twenty years lying and cheating to help make you rich. I was trying to outwit you, Papa, but I guess I couldn't do it." More than in earlier plays the characters describe one another: Marcus says of John Bagtry: "A foolish man, an empty man from an idiot world. A man who wants nothing but war, any war, just a war. A man who believes in nothing, and never will. A man in space—"

The speech of the characters is more obviously Southern than the speech in *The Little Foxes*. Hellman accomplishes this less by using dialect than with idioms and rhythms. Within the general pattern each major character speaks differently. Birdie speaks with the broken rhythms we heard in *The Little Foxes*. Lavinia's speech is fragmented, vague. Oscar is whiney, rapid, jerky, as we remember him from the earlier play. When he discovers Regina has bought new clothes, he says, "You really gone crazy? Nobody's ever worn furs in this climate since old lady Somers put that bear rug around her and jumped out the porch." When Regina says she didn't ask how much the clothes cost, Oscar says, shrilly, "Didn't even ask? Didn't even ask? You gone real crazy, acting like Miss Vanderbilt, whatever her name is—rich people up North don't act that way." Marcus speaks rather formally, is as distant with his sons as with strangers.

So once again we find an ironic play, a demonstration of lovelessness begetting lovelessness, and a clear, perhaps overly clear demonstration of how the loveless got that way. Once again, Hellman used the Jonsonian, Machiavellian device of the "trickster tricked." And once again the critics misunderstood. In fact, the

Time reviewer said that "tricking-the-trickster" would be appropriate for a "cold, hard comedy" but not for *Another Part of the Forest*
(Dec. 2, 1946, p. 56). Hellman did not write another original play
for five years. When she did, it was, to critics, more obviously
ironic, with ten major characters and an ending that no one liked,
and with a plot that was, for the most part, misunderstood. Hellman
had good reason for finally deciding she was through with the
theater.

CHAPTER 4

The Plays of the 1950s and 1960s

I The Autumn Garden

An autumn garden is one which by winter time will fade and not be a garden any more. It's a chrysanthemum garden. The people in the play are coming into the winter of life.

—Lillian Hellman

Somebody told me once that when something's been wrong with you and it gets cured, you miss it very much at first.

—The Searching Wind

THE time is September 1949; the place, "a town on the Gulf of Mexico, a hundred miles from New Orleans." Six people are paying summer guests at the home of Constance Tuckerman. Most of them grew up together. Frederick Ellis is engaged to Constance's niece, Sophie, the daughter of Constance's late brother Sam and a French woman he married before World War II. After the war Constance brought Sophie to America. Frederick's mother, Carrie Ellis, grew up with Constance, as did Edward Crossman, an alcoholic bank clerk who supposedly has been in love with Constance for years.

Although the Ellises are rich, Frederick's grandmother, Mrs. Mary Ellis, controls the money. Also spending the summer are retired army general Benjamin Griggs and his flirtatious, pathetically silly wife Rose. Griggs wants a divorce, but Rose ignores his demand. They expectantly await the arrival of the Denerys. Nick Denery, dilettante artist and Constance's old beau, jilted Constance to marry a rich woman and has never returned since he went to Europe to study art.

When Nick arrives, he meddles in everyone's life. He tells Carrie Ellis that Payson, a man with whom Frederick spends all his time, is homosexual. He tells Rose to visit a doctor. When she does, she discovers that her hypochondria has masked real heart trouble. He tells Constance that Crossman has always loved her. He gets drunk and puts Sophie in a compromising situation. As a result of his meddling, all the characters are confronted with truths about themselves, but their life-long patterns cannot be broken. Griggs will stay with Rose and come to "like her even less." Frederick will remain a mama's boy and never marry. Crossman, realizing he has been lying to himself for many years about wanting Constance, will go on drinking. Constance, finally seeing through her idealized Nick, is left to "keep on keepin' on." Sophie, young and realistic, escapes, finally able to return to Europe with money Mrs. Denery has given her to compensate for Nick's behavior, money Sophie insists on calling a blackmail payment to make the Denerys see Nick's behavior for what it is.

Prior to the New York opening, director Harold Clurman said he felt that much more "happens" in *The Autumn Garden* than in *The Little Foxes*, but that Hellman took "care to make it seem less." He said, "She not only wants a greater semblance to the casual flow of life, but is trying to say something about the norm of things. . . . Miss Hellman's play is anti-sentimental, anti-fuzzy-mindedness. Too many nice people . . . play blind-man's buff with reality for want of a sense of direction. . . . They do not realize that all the moments of their lives add up to a sum for which they must be prepared to pay an irrevocable price. . . . To escape this realization most of us lie to ourselves with pretty words. . . . In Miss Hellman's terms, most of us are earnest without being serious" (*HT*, Mar. 4, 1951).

The disparity between earnestness and seriousness is evidently important to Hellman. The contrast occurs more than once in her work and in interviews. She elaborated on it to Harry Gilroy: "If you are inwardly a serious person, . . . in the middle years it will pay off. . . . You can be frivolous . . . and still be serious. I mean serious emotionally and intellectually. Many people who pretend to be really serious aren't at all. It is not a matter of being interested in serious problems—you might devote all your time to milking cows and still be intrinsically serious. It is not a matter of what you have accomplished, either; yet an artist who isn't serious shows it in any work he does, and conversely nothing really good can be done by someone who isn't serious" (*NYT*, Feb. 25, 1951).

Clurman's summary of the theme echoes a key speech in the last scene of *The Autumn Garden*, a speech Clurman specifically asked

Hellman to write, apparently feeling that the theme should be stated directly: "So at any given moment you're only the sum of your life up to then. There are no big moments you can reach unless you've a pile of smaller moments to stand on. That big hour of decision, the turning point in your life, the someday you've counted on when you'd suddenly wipe out your past mistakes, do the work you'd never done, think the way you'd never thought, have what you'd never had—it just doesn't come suddenly. You've trained yourself for it while you waited—or you've let it all run past you and frittered yourself away."

Reviews were mixed. Although many reviewers described *The Autumn Garden* as a comedy and spoke of the laughter and the wit in the dialogue, they also found the play pessimistic and depressing, an effect Hellman had not intended. Harry Gilroy, summing up Hellman's comments, wrote, "It [middle age] is a time of life when one has had a chance to try all one's capacities, felt the emotions of life, known love. One has the powers to enjoy life in any way that is preferred. At the same time, one can always have the additional pleasure of being reflective about experiences." Hellman added that the play wasn't "meant to say that people can't do anything about" their empty lives. "It is meant to say the opposite—they can do a great deal with their lives. . . . I don't like cheerless plays," she said. "I don't feel cheerless about the world" (*NYT*, Feb. 25, 1951).

Perhaps some of the intended cheerfulness leaked out of the play during rehearsal. Hellman was disturbed that "something was happening to the play, life was going out of it, which can and does happen on the stage and once started can seldom be changed" (*UW*, p. 268). Cheerful or cheerless, the play was the occasion for some reviewers to attack Hellman's alleged political bias.

The *Christian Science Monitor* review is typical: "'The Autumn Garden' is an unfairly slanted representation of American life. If produced abroad, it may handily serve the Kremlin's determined campaign to convince Europe that life in the United States is preponderantly decadent" (Mar. 17, 1951). Most reviewers invoked the dramatic shade of Chekhov, and *The Autumn Garden* is in many respects Chekhovian, though the resemblance lies in the ironic treatment.

In Hellman's work one finds characters who in a sense stand apart from the action and provide moral judgment on it. They, like the author, are ironists. In *The Autumn Garden* the ironists are Crossman, an observer whose detachment is shown not only in the

tone and content of his dialogue but in his usual physical isolation on
the side porch, drink in hand, and Mrs. Ellis, set apart by her age
and wealth, an intelligent old lady who "is broken and senile when
she wishes to be broken and senile."

Sophie, too, is an outsider, with her values already formed when
she comes to America. She tells Constance, "I have not been happy,
and I cannot continue here. I cannot be what you have wished me to
be, and I do not want the world you want for me. It is too late—"
Constance says, "Too late? You were thirteen years old when you
came here," and Sophie replies, "I came from another world and in
that world thirteen is not young." (Act II, Scene 2, p. 538) When
asked if she had been happy at home, Sophie says that she does not
"think in such words," adding that she was comfortable with herself
there and is no longer. Hellman may be suggesting here that we too
should not think in such words.

Most of the characters in *The Autumn Garden* are, as critic Alan
Downer says, "deluded romantics," and Sophie's "struggles to play
her assigned role in the romantic drama the others have chosen to
enact are by turns funny, pathetic, and shockingly pointed." [1] But
Sophie is not an ironist. She is a clear-eyed realist. She loses no
illusions during the course of the play because she has no illusions to
lose.

Illusions, however, cobweb the minds of the other characters. A
news item of the time tells us that the working title of *The Autumn
Garden* was "Five or Six Kinds of Love," but the romantic conflicts
in the play are secondary to the main theme, which is, once again,
the harm we do ourselves and those we claim to love through
self-deception. (Clurman may have been wrong about the theme
and wrong in asking for Griggs's speech. The real theme, self-
deception, is certainly expressed in a number of shorter speeches.)
To the degree that they deceive themselves, these people are at
best a nuisance; at their worst, they are destructive to those close to
them, like the fools in the novels of Henry James, whose muddled
behavior makes life difficult for his protagonists.

Mrs. Griggs exists on social gabble and gossip. Gregariousness
keeps her "young" and "gay," two words she uses more than once in
the play. Having no inner life, she lives off the lives of others. Nick,
too, lives off other people's emotions, although he is more active
than Rose Griggs. In *The Autumn Garden* he is the ironic catalyst.
The play turns on Nick's awaited arrival and its consequences. More
actively than similar Chekhov characters, Nick provokes the

decisions and revelations that force the other characters into at least a momentary recognition of the waste in their lives.

The ironists, Crossman and Grandma Ellis, see through him immediately. When Nick says that Constance sacrificed her life for her brother, Crossman says, "Nick is still a Southerner. With us every well-born lady sacrifices her life for something: a man, a house, sometimes a gardenia bush." (Act I, pp. 481-82) Nick says, "We loved each other so very much. Remember, Ned?" Crossman replies that he doesn't "remember that much love." (Act I, p. 483) When Nick says that he has heard that Crossman drinks too much, saying, "I hope you didn't mind, Ned," Crossman says, "Not a bit. I want to know about you, too. Ever had syphilis, Nick? Kind of thing one has to know right off, if you understand me." (Act I, p. 483) Crossman finally tells him, "You are just exactly the way I remember you. And that I wouldn't have believed of any man." (Act II, Scene 2, p. 517)

When Nick, bored and restless, asks Mrs. Ellis whether he will enjoy reading at her age (he can't divert Sophie from reading to her), Mrs. Ellis says, "No, Mr. Denery. If you haven't learned to read at your age, you won't learn at mine." (Act II, Scene 2, p. 508) Nick puts his hand on her shoulder; shrugging it off, she says, "And you're a toucher: you constantly touch people or lean on them. Little moments of sensuality. One should have sensuality whole or not at all. . . . There are many of you: the touchers and the leaners." (Act II, Scene 2, p. 509)

The romantics, seeing Nick as he wishes to be seen or as they wish to see him, allow him to alter the static situations they have lived in comfortably for years. The plot does not, as some critics seemed to think, turn on the Nick-Sophie sofa incident, but on Nick's meddling. He commits Hawthorne's "unpardonable sin"; he deliberately manipulates other human beings for his own amusement.

The visual symbol of his manipulation in *The Autumn Garden* is his new painting of Constance, dressed in a cheap dress he bought at a Negro store, which makes her look much older and less attractive than she is. This painting shows not the real Constance, but the real Nick, as Constance finally realizes when she sees it. The youthful painting Constance has kept all these years as the "only important thing" she has, as a symbol of their "romantic love," is as false as the new one in a different sense.

Nick's feeding off others' lives is revealed in the action of the play

through his interaction with each subgroup of characters. Nick tells
Carrie that Fred is involved with a known homosexual. Her reaction
causes Fred to learn that Payson has cared nothing for him. Nick
tells Constance that Crossman has always loved her. Acting on this
misinformation, Constance causes Crossman to face his own
self-deception, a self-deception he takes hard because he has seen
through that of others.

Nick counsels Mrs. Griggs to see a heart specialist. Her visit
forces her to face what she has suspected but has refused to
acknowledge. She then has a moment of self-knowledge, but we
know her well enough by this time to know that her promise to
Griggs to give him a divorce in a year will be forgotten and life will
go on as before for her. The knowledge of her heart condition forces
Griggs in turn to face the possibility that he never really wanted
freedom, that he is all used up. Nick's drunken behavior with
Sophie precipitates another revelation for Constance, who not only
sees Nick for the first time for what he truly is, but learns that
Sophie has always wanted to go home. Since even Crossman has
deceived himself to some extent, only Sophie and Mrs. Ellis are left
unharmed by Nick's behavior. Sophie, in fact, benefits. Sophie
(whose name means wisdom) has worn a mask and can now remove
it.

The others must face what they have permanently become
through their habitual actions or inaction. Crossman earlier has
warned Sophie that it can happen to her, too. "For God's sake,
Sophie, have an opinion about *something*. . . . You're beginning to
talk wise, cautious—the very highest form of American talk. . . .
You've been busy cultivating a pseudostupidity. Another five years
and you won't be *pseudo*stupid." If Crossman is right about her
probable future, Nick's foolishness saves her from it.

Sophie's refusal to take money from Nina unless it is called
blackmail, not a charitable gift, is an important fact, misunderstood
by many reviewers. Sophie does not suddenly change character.
Her conversations with Crossman, brief as they are, let us know her
true character. She is not a blackmailer like the count in *Watch on
the Rhine*, as some critics have understood her to be. She wants
Nina and Nick, who have "too many words for simple things," to
face Nick's behavior for what it is: not cute, boyish, and charming,
but ugly. Sophie tells Nina, "You wish to be the kind lady who most
honorably stays to discharge—within reason—her obligations. And
who goes off, as she has gone off many other times, to make the

reconciliation with her husband. How would you and Mr. Denery go on living without such incidents as me? I have been able to give you a second, or a twentieth, honeymoon." (Act III, p. 538) To Sophie the word "blackmail" represents "more than a way of calling something."

Chekhov's characters typically are not changed permanently by the events of the play; neither are Hellman's. Griggs and Rose will go on as before; so will the Ellises. Crossman will go on drinking. Nick will continue to make messes which Nina will clean up. Their reliving their past experiences does not change their futures; the end of the play leaves one with the feeling that their pasts and their futures are contained in their present, and their present is ongoing. In the words of the Gershwin song, they will do, do, do what they've done, done, done before.

One ends with this judgment of the characters because Hellman has used Sophie, Crossman, and Mrs. Ellis to control the audience's attitudes toward the other characters and their situations. As G. C. Sedgewick says in *Of Irony: Especially in Drama*, "The ironic control that a spectator has over a play before him is a matter both of his superior knowledge and of his attitude of mind as evoked by this knowledge or by some other source of suggestion." [2]

The audience's understanding of the dramatic action in *The Autumn Garden* is more involved than that of the characters. Although particular characters may report the results of offstage actions, the characters most affected by this information learn of it after the audience does. Fred, for example, learns after the audience of Nick's conversation with his mother about Payson. The audience learns before Griggs of his wife's visit to the heart specialist. Not only does the audience have superior knowledge in this direct sense, but the spectators understand the import of the characters' speeches better than do the characters themselves. As Siegfried Melchinger says of Chekhov's dialogue, when people in *The Autumn Garden* talk, the truth is in what they don't say, or in what they don't hear themselves and others say: "they talk past each other." [3] There is an incongruity between things as the audience knows them really to be and things as they are believed to be by the characters.

The contrast between the reality of a situation and the illusions of the characters produces comic incongruity. Understanding the tone and attitude of the playwright, many critics called *The Autumn Garden* a comedy, although Marvin Felheim wrote an essay about the Chekhovian elements in the play, treating it as a tragedy. Behind such a comparison lies an assumption about Chekhov. We must remember that Chekhov called some of his plays comedies and that, as Hellman says of his work, we too often "know only something that we call 'Chekhovian,' and by that we mean a stage filled with sweet, soupy, frustrated people, created by a man who wept for their fate," so that Chekhovian has come to mean "a world filled with puff-ball people lying on a dusty table waiting for a wind to roll them off." Out of, Hellman says, the "need that shallow people have for emotional fancy dress, their desire to deck out ordinary trouble in gaudy colors, and to teeter around life like children in their mother's high-heeled shoes," [4] Chekhov created comedy. And so did Hellman.

All of the characters in *The Autumn Garden* except Frederick, Sophie, and Mrs. Ellis are middle-class Americans in the middle of the journeys of their lives. They started out to be one thing and have ended up another without realizing it, or they delude themselves that some day they will be what they dream of being. They cling to a vanished youth and charm, like Nick and Mrs. Griggs, or they tell themselves that life would be different had their separate dreams come true: Griggs would have been a scholar; Constance, Nick's beloved and the inspiration for his painting; Crossman, happily married to Constance.

They come to the summer home, where most of them have grown up, and reach the end of a summer season, in the year 1949 and in their lives. They bring with them the real past and that past colored by memory, and in the real present they lose their romantic futures.* They are children playing at being grown-ups. And in that summer house where most of them have spent a part of their childhood, where all of them have gathered for the past seven summers, moving into their middle age together, they become an ironic demonstration of Chekhov's belief that "a reasoned life without a definite outlook is not a life, but a burden and a horror." [5]

Some critics complained that Hellman gave them no character representing the norm. The norm is the mind and attitude of the playwright revealed in the play, an attitude consistent with the rest of her work. In *The Little Foxes* the guilty are the people who stand around and watch; in *The Searching Wind*, the people who let Hitler happen; in *Days to Come*, those so blind to the consequences of their private actions that they make possible the strikebreaking and its violence. In *The Children's Hour*, the guilty are the "unco guid" who give a child's lie the power to destroy; in *Toys in the Attic*, those who can't see the real motivations for their actions; in the memoirs, people who refuse to take the responsibility for their own actions, who won't stand up and be counted when the test comes.

Hellman says more than once, directly or through her characters, that we must do our best. We use that phrase so often as an excuse, an apology for not having done our best, that we miss the force of it in Hellman. She is a humanist, and the call to do one's very best is a high challenge. The characters in *The Autumn Garden* fail to meet that challenge. Mrs. Ellis copes with loneliness in her own way. Perhaps, this late in life, she does her best. And Sophie, unhappy in America, does her best. (When Sophie tells Crossman that she has wanted to go home for five years but has found no way, so has decided to "do the best [she] can," Crossman repeats, "as if he were moved," "The best you can?" Sophie responds, "I think so. Maybe you've never tried to do that, Mr. Ned. Maybe none of you have tried.")

Given the limitations of character and circumstance, very few of us truly do our best. Perhaps recognition of this failure causes many critics to accuse Hellman of pessimism. Chekhov, too, has been called a pessimist. Hellman says of this charge, "I do not understand the pessimist theory. I know of no writer who ever made it more clear that he believed in the future. There is every difference between sadness and despair." [6]

Hellman once said, "If I did not hope to grow, I would not hope to live" (*Six Plays*, p. xii). The characters in *The Autumn Garden* have stopped growing. Nick is the perpetual amateur artist, the professional "young man," the eternally "promising youth." Rose Griggs still employs the flirtatiousness appropriate to a Southern debutante. They are all caught in repetitive patterns, although Nick and Rose refuse to recognize the repetition. They are what they have always been, what they will always be. The differences are in degree.

Griggs and Crossman know what they have come to be and will be. And they know how it happened. There is no one person or outside force to blame. Griggs says: "Most people like us haven't done anything to themselves; they've let it be done to them. I had no right to let it be done to me, but I let it be done. What consolation can I find in not having made myself any more useless than an Ellis, a Denery, a Tuckerman?"

Constance's future is the most problematic and for that reason the most interesting. She learns, and "all in one day," as Zan might have said, that her romantic notions about Nick were false, that her dreams for Sophie were false, that her old beau is a beau no longer. We sense that these people won't gather at the old summer house again. What will happen to Constance, stripped of her illusions? Although for the rest of the characters the play gives a pattern of a future repetitive of the past, Sophie is freed, and Constance is left hanging. Perhaps it is Constance's "discoveries" with no resolution that have caused directors who apparently dislike an equal emphasis upon multiple characters to attempt to make her the central character.

Reviews indicate that the director of an English television production of *The Autumn Garden* in 1960 attempted to make Constance the central figure, as did the director of a performance on New York's Channel 13 in 1966. She is not the central character, however; the central "character" is the theme, symbolized by the house and the groupings within it.

Hellman uses social occasions to show us sides of a character that appear only on those occasions. The curtain opens on a grouping. It comes down on a house empty, visually, save for Constance and Crossman, who will soon be gone, and we are left, reflectively, looking at an empty house, to which summer will come no more. A searching wind has blown through it, scattering the characters before it.

Critics often complained that Hellman's plots don't develop until the second act. In *The Autumn Garden*, as in *Watch on the Rhine* and *Toys in the Attic*, Hellman uses the leisurely first act to establish atmosphere and the attitude she wishes the audience to take toward the characters and situation. Hellman uses subgroupings, duets between characters to advance the action; that is, to strip the characters of their illusions. Illustrating the interplay of these subgroups would, however, require virtually line-by-line explication of the play.

We learn what life is typically like for these characters before the arrival of the catalytic character. We are given our point of view, that of Crossman and Mrs. Ellis, the ironists, who are "both in and out of the game," in Whitman's phrase; that is, both participants in the action, yet spectators. The ironists' comments distance the audience. Hellman gives us the feeling that the ironic characters are speaking to us, the audience. (While Hellman employs "playacting" by characters in both *The Little Foxes* and *The Autumn Garden*, they wear their motley with a difference: the foxes perform for one another; the ironists in *The Autumn Garden* for the audience.)

We learn from the first act that the characters come from similar backgrounds; they thus share a code of manners, a way of life. Yet each character is an individual. The groupings and regroupings allow us to see the differences caused by age, wealth, sex, class. In a sense, they are all middle class or upper middle class. Yet Rose is "new rich," hence different from the others. Sophie, in an inversion of Henry James, is a European who has learned to survive and adapt by facing realities as the Americans are unable to do. Nick, though he spent his childhood with these people, has been "Europe-anized."

Act II gives us Nick in action, meddling in everyone's life. This meddling apparently gives rise to many subplots, and critics spoke of the many plots in *The Autumn Garden*; yet what Hellman gives us is not really plot, but pattern. Each character lives out a situation similar to the others' in a different way.

In *The Autumn Garden* the number of people involved in repetitions of the central pattern further distances the audience, adding to the ironic effect. In ironic demonstration we do not empathize; we understand. As these individuals and groups move before us, we look for what they have in common, and we discover, as always in a Hellman play, that these people are defeated by their own "life-lies," not by life.

Many critics, looking at the number of characters and situations in *The Autumn Garden*, described the play as having the density of a novel. If we pursue the analogy, we discover that Hellman's treatment of the action in *The Autumn Garden* differs from that of her earlier plays. Although she had in the past employed the "messenger element" on occasion, in *The Autumn Garden* she employs this device often to tell us about events that a novel or a "plotty" play would show us. On stage we see the *inner life* of the characters, the emotional results of the offstage events.

We never meet Payson. Offstage, Frederick reads proof with him, buys him a ticket to Europe. Carrie confronts him offstage. He dismisses Frederick offstage. Sophie learns from Frederick that Payson is through with him, in an exchange we don't see. Ned and Nick have a drinking bout together offstage. The Ellises and Rose attend a party, where Rose has a "sinking spell." Crossman, Griggs, and Nina spend a whole Sunday together on a picnic at Pass Christian. Rose visits her brother and a heart specialist.

The Autumn Garden is the only successful Hellman play for which there is no movie version, perhaps because she was blacklisted at the time of its production or just because it was too subtle for Hollywood. If one reads the play thinking in terms of a film script, one sees that all these reported actions could be successfully developed into scenes. Hellman deliberately pared down in order to concentrate on the effects. Interviewer Richard Stern said to her "the other day you were talking about *Autumn Garden. . . .* At least, you gave its technical source: you said you wanted to write a novel in that form and then you talked about the subject matter of the play as if it were a sort of after-effect of the technique" (*Contact*, p. 114).

The structure of this play is anticlimactic. Scenes are interrupted; curtains are slow and reflective. We know from her other plays how easy it would have been for Hellman to write "big" confrontation scenes. It is their absence, the lack of the typical Hellman "charge," of which some critics complained.

The Autumn Garden is a comedy of anticlimax, of denial of expectations. No one marries, no one dies, no one is moved to some horrendously final act. Audiences might have been happier had Constance and Ned agreed to marry, but that would have violated the pattern. (One wonders if, in some preliminary version, they *did* come together.)

The use of a pattern, of multiple characters demonstrating the same theme, leads, once again, to a play without a protagonist. In *The Autumn Garden* Hellman gives us an attitude rather than a central character with which to identify.

Hellman believes in decency, intelligence, will, as opposed to moral inertia and irresponsibility. She believes that we must do our best, our human best; we must not fool ourselves or other people, we must strive to grow; we must be "committed" in the existential sense of that term. In her plays and in her memoirs Hellman uses again and again the phrase "in space." A person who speaks or acts "in space" has no commitment, no reasoned outlook; he is like a kite without a string.

John Gassner said of Hellman's play in the 1950s, "It contained some half dozen excellently drawn characters (this itself was an unusual achievement in the decade's theatre), as well as some of the most incisive and revealing dialogue of which this vigorous playwright was capable. The play also included a measure of human sympathy, rare in a Hellman trial . . . as well as a degree of affecting indirection and stasis unusual for a writer who had usually favored overt conflicts on the stage." [7] He had, however, reservations, which were shared by enough reviewers to limit the play's success.

The Autumn Garden ran for only 101 performances, a barely successful run, since on Broadway one hundred performances is the minimum below which a play is considered a failure. Hellman called it at the time her "most satisfying play—certainly . . . in the writing." Of the box office, she said, "We'll have to do $17,000 to $18,000 weekly . . . to live. If we do it, fine, but if we don't that doesn't mean that 'Autumn Garden' is any less of a play." She said that *The Autumn Garden* "started as a comedy" and that there was no central character (*WTS*, Mar. 3, 1951). In an interview in 1965, asked which of her plays she "liked best," she answered, "I suppose *Autumn Garden*. I suppose I think it is the best play, if that is what you mean by 'like' " (*WW*, p. 120).

The play has received little critical attention since 1951. John Gassner in *Theatre at the Crossroads* repeated his puzzlement about what Hellman was for, blaming some of the difficulty on her "tough-fibred resolution." He concluded, however, "Comprehensiveness did not lessen her power and a compassionate viewpoint would not blunt the edge of her writing. *The Autumn Garden*, in 1951, spoke better for her than for the decade. The power and edge of her writing remained generally intact, this time without the possibility of provoking the charge of melodrama." [8] Alan Downer said, "In a number of ways this is Miss Hellman's most original play. Structurally, it escapes from the technical slickness which has been by turns the wonder and despair of her critics. . . . Humanely, it reveals the nature of our life, of our means of grace. . . . Thus the play presents an almost Chekhovian image of society, never denying the chaos through which we move, but by the subtlest shaping and selection creating an order within the chaos and lending meaning to experience." He concluded, "Were it not utter foolishness to call so experienced a talent as Miss Hellman's promising, it would be proper to say that *The Autumn Garden* was the most promising play of the year." [9]

John Mason Brown quotes Crossman's big closing speech, saying, "I quote these sentences in which a character not only reveals his inner anguishes but summarizes his spiritual autobiography because they are symptomatic. They indicate how Miss Hellman's interest has shifted from outward climaxes to inward crises." He says that her characters may "be more numerous than necessary, [but] they are shrewdly observed by a wise woman who is writing a play which, in spite of its faults, is in many ways the most mature and probing to have come from her gifted pen" (*SR*, Mar. 31, 1951, pp. 28–29).

Marvin Felheim finds the realism of *The Autumn Garden* to be to the "essence of human existence, not to the representation of life." He says the characters behave in a manner that we call Chekhovian because Hellman lets them "alone to act out their destinies, regarding them only with love and understanding; in her earlier play, she took sides. . . . In *The Autumn Garden*, she does not make this kind of break-down. The result is true complexity, both in dialectics and mechanics." He contends that the drama is "not merely psychological (as in Tennessee Williams) nor sociological (as in Arthur Miller) but it is artistic (poetic) and moral—and all in the Chekhovian sense." A reading of the play supports Felheim's contention, but does not necessarily support his conclusion that "the kind of drama we have in *The Autumn Garden* is the only kind which makes for modern tragedy." [10] It may be the kind which makes for modern "serious comedy."

Jacob Adler finds that "the play works, though it was not altogether successful on Broadway. Miss Hellman's dialogue and characterization survive her shift in technique quite well. She succeeds, like Chekhov, in keeping us interested in these people. . . . She succeeds in making her point that most people have insufficient will. And she succeeds in making it a point of universal validity. . . . Yet that playwright is rare who can follow where Chekhov trod. . . . There is little positive evil in *The Autumn Garden*, only weakness; and it may be for this reason that the play lacks the power and drive of Miss Hellman at her best." [11]

Reading the criticism, one finds that invoking the name of Chekhov did invite the invidious comparisons John Gassner had warned against, and these proved misleading because Hellman was not attempting to write like Chekhov and failing. The themes, the irony, the technique were present in her work long before *The Autumn Garden*.

By her own testimony, she had always been more interested in novels than in plays and had always, with the exception of *The*

Children's Hour, an atypical play, taken a novelist's view of her characters. *The Autumn Garden* is the culmination of earlier attempts at the novelistic technique, differing from them in the degree to which she perfected the technique of walking away from the big scene and giving us only the emotional effects of it.

Hellman thinks this play her best; most critics choose *The Little Foxes*. Thinking of Wallace Stevens' "Thirteen Ways of Looking at a Blackbird," one could argue that, if one prefers the blackbird's singing, *i.e.*, exhilaration, one chooses *The Little Foxes*; if one prefers the moment after, *i.e.*, amused contemplation and reflection, one chooses *The Autumn Garden*.

The play was not revived until 1976. Lee Strasberg blamed the original production for most of the faults critics found with the play. Strasberg said:

Its seeming indirectness was intended to place the emphasis on the characters, on their inner conflicts and relationships rather than the outward drama. . . . The play was well done, but in a style more suited to the earlier plays. The characters ceased to exist when they left the stage. When they returned, their reappearance seemed unmotivated. The characters described their experiences rather than re-creating them. They seemed to 'act' rather than to live. An almost 'Chekhovian' environment was needed to be created, one that would permit a sense of continuous action with the characters continuing to live and behave after their dialogue stopped. The setting would have had to be more open to permit action to go on while other people were speaking, and thus to create a kind of symphonic orchestration of the behavior and the attitudes of the people. A production visualized along these lines would have served to bring out the inherent humaneness of the characters . . . and their inability to act would have been dramatized on the stage.[12]

In 1976 the Long Wharf Theater in New Haven revived *The Autumn Garden*, and the second time around at least one critic, Walter Kerr, understood the niece: "[The niece] is, after all, a girl of spirit and considerable independence. She wants no favors, will accept nothing like charity. . . . The girl is both serious and wry." And in Kerr's final judgment of *The Autumn Garden*, "The play itself emerges, at long last, as one of Miss Hellman's very best. Fresh recognition of its qualities has been overdue for some time; in taking such care with the work's nuances, the Long Wharf has arrived at an evening in the theater that is well-nigh perfect" (*NYT*, Nov. 28, 1976). Miss Hellman's faith in her play is vindicated after a quarter of a century.

II   Toys in the Attic

Most of us lie to ourselves.—*The Autumn Garden*

If I did not hope to grow, I would not hope to live.
—Introduction to *Six Plays*

The place is New Orleans; the time, indeterminate. The Berniers sisters still have an ice box when other people have refrigerators; people in the play take trains, not planes.

Anna and Carrie Berniers have always sacrificed themselves for their feckless younger brother Julian. Through the years they have talked and dreamed of going to Europe, but always, when they have saved a little money, Julian has needed it. Living for him has become a way of life.

Julian suddenly turns up with Lily, his bride of a year, rich and bringing gifts including the paid-up mortgage to the house the sisters hate and tickets for the long-postponed trip to Europe. With the help of his ex-lover Mrs. Warkins, Julian has bought land vital to a money-making project of Cyrus Warkins, a rich and dangerous man.

Lily's rich mother, Albertine Prine, lives with her black chauffeur, Henry Simpson. Carrie overhears the two of them discussing the fact that Mrs. Warkins is Henry's cousin. From Lily's talk she puts facts together and manipulates the confused girl into calling Warkins and telling him that his wife is part Negro and is behind Julian's land deal. Carrie does all this instinctively, without real forethought, because she can't bear to see Julian independent of her. Anna has accused her of incestuous feelings for him.

Julian has gone to give Mrs. Warkins her share of the money. They are met by Warkins' thugs, who slash her face, beat up Julian, and take the money. When he comes home bruised, beaten, and broke, Carrie is happy. Lily's mother knows that someday Carrie will turn Julian against Lily by letting him know about Lily's phone call to Warkins. Lily will come home to her, and Henry will leave because Lily hates him. Anna, who has seen the truth about all of them and had planned to go to Europe without Carrie, will take her job back and continue to be a mother to her sister and brother, knowing what she knows and living with the knowledge.

For *Toys in the Attic*, her eighth and last original play, Hellman received the New York Drama Critics' Circle award for the best play of the 1960 season. The Pulitzer Drama Jury selected *Toys in the Attic* for the Pulitzer Prize, but was overruled by the Advisory Board, which gave the award to the musical *Fiorello!*

While working on *Toys in the Attic*, Hellman told Richard Stern that she felt something was giving her trouble: "It may be that the idea for the play is almost too good. It sounds whacky to say but somewhere it's a little too neat. I've never had neat ideas before." [13] At the time she was midway through the second act. The time of the action then was around 1912.

She considered Lily's mother the second most important character and worried that she was taking over the play. One difference between Hellman's concept then and the final development of the plot lies in the character of Henry, Mrs. Prine's chauffeur. In the final version Henry is Mrs. Prine's lover (this plot thread is based on Hellman's Aunt Lily and her chauffeur), but in the Stern interview he "doesn't like the woman he works for very much, but she pays him well. And she interests him." Hellman interrupted herself to say that she did not think the play would be written that way, and it wasn't.

During the Boston tryout performances, Hellman said:

I suppose I wanted to say a number of things. I think I wanted to say that not all kinds of love—so-called love—are noble and good, that there's much in love that's destructive, including the love that holds up false notions of success, of the acquisition of money.

Asked if the characters were based on people she knew, Hellman said,

There was a man I knew years ago, a sort of friend of my father's; if there's any real character in the play, he is the one. I always felt if people had let him alone, or if he'd had the strength to ignore everybody's standards, which most of us don't have, he'd have been a wholly different man.

I always remember he told me one night how much he loved horses and how he wanted to spend his life around them. Instead, his sister and his wife's family told him he should go into business. He did and he failed in business and he failed as a man. I felt very sorry for him. I guess that's what the play says, too, to live by your own standards, even if you're going to be lonely and unpopular. I don't think you always come out lonely. A couple of people I know have come out as well as anybody else, and in some cases far better (*NYT*, Feb. 21, 1960).

Readers of *Pentimento* and *An Unfinished Woman* know that the two sisters of *Toys in the Attic* derive in part from Hellman's aunts, Jenny and Hannah (Anna was called Hannah in the early drafts), in the sense that Hellman saw the same kind of role-reversal in them that she portrays in *Toys in the Attic*. In *Pentimento* she writes, "I suppose all women living together take on what we think of as male and female roles, but my aunts had made a rather puzzling mix-about. Jenny, who was the prettier, the softer in face and manner, had assumed a confidence she didn't have, and had taken on, demanded, I think, the practical, less pleasant duties. Hannah, who had once upon a time been more intelligent than Jenny, had somewhere given over, and although she held the official job, a very good one in those days of underpaid ladies, of secretary to the president of a large corporation, it was Jenny who called the tunes for their life together" (pp. 12–13).

She described the sisters of the play: "Two quite nice women who have been devoted to each other and to their brother, peaceful and relatively happy. By the end of the play neither likes the other and the bright one finds she has been bored by the not bright one, and they've been in competition for the brother's affection under a very polite guise; neither has ever told the truth about anything. Not that they've lied, but they've just never seen the truth about any-thing." [14]

Hellman's father, like Julian, failed in the shoe business because he was cheated by his partner. Hellman's Uncle Willy was, like Julian, happier hunting and fishing in the bayou. The offstage villain, though a lawyer-businessman, apparently has connections with the underworld. In early drafts his name was Scarlatti, and one remembers Hellman's girlhood glimpse of New Orleans Mafia affairs as related in *Pentimento*.

The story of Carrie and Julian eating their meals on the back steps is an incident from Hellman's own childhood. And the character of Lily, whom she intended to be "not crazy, but fey, and disjointed, and sweet and lost" may be a little of Hellman as a girl, a little of her mother.

Mrs. Prine is like Hellman's Aunt Lily only in her relationship with the chauffeur. When *Toys in the Attic* was published, Hellman had a letter from her aunt's son, asking whether she had meant Mrs. Prine "to be his mother and her fancy man to be Peters." Hellman had not realized till then, she says, that "the seeds of Mrs. Prine had, indeed, flown from Aunt Lily's famous gardenias to another kind of garden" (*P*, p. 86). But the character sounds like the mature Hellman herself a great deal of the time, and sometimes the tone is that of Sophronia as Hellman has described her in the memoirs.

Although one can trace the "seeds" of her characters in *Toys in the Attic* more specifically because of Hellman's memoirs, they are, of course, fully imagined creations, autobiographical only in the sense that, as Hellman said, "everybody [a writer knows] is in every play."

With the exception of the Pulitzer Board of Trustees, there was general agreement that *Toys in the Attic* was a fine play. A few critics thought it Hellman's best, but most believed *The Little Foxes* surpassed it. The principal reservations concerned the fancied resemblance to Tennessee Williams' work, the structure of the first act, and the references to incest and miscegenation.

With a New Orleans setting and explicit sexual references, the comparison with Williams' work was perhaps inevitable. Marya Mannes raised the comparison, making the point that "economy and discipline" distinguish Hellman's work from Williams's. She added that both Hellman and Williams deal with "unlovely or painful states of being," but Hellman's characters are so three-dimensional, "even to the extent of being often funny," that there is no sense of "gratuitous shock" as in Williams's work. She concluded that Hellman's "is the more consistent integrity: she will do nothing for effect alone, although she well knows how." [15]

Toys in the Attic, like *Watch on the Rhine* and *The Autumn Garden*, received some criticism for a slow first act, but even those who found it slow agreed with Brooks Atkinson: "Miss Hellman's talents reap their rewards—her talent for original characterizations, her hard-headed knowledge of the intricacies of human relationships and her realism about the meanings of life" (*NYT*, Feb. 26, 1960).

As Richard Watts said, "Everything appears so pleasant and friendly at the start. . . . One advantage of this slow, friendly beginning is, of course, that the growing revelation of the ugly passions . . . becomes the more shocking as they unfold. But there is another virtue of this sort of deliberate opening. It is that, by the time you are faced with the secret horrors seething within them, you feel you know so much about all the characters that there is something inherently dramatic in the discovery that what you have seen is nothing more than their surfaces" (*Post*, Feb. 26, 1960).

Wolcott Gibbs, in praising the play, expressed a reservation indicating a misunderstanding of the play's true theme. Subject matter and plot are not necessarily identical with theme, as one sees in an analysis of *Toys in the Attic*. Gibbs said, "The trouble with 'Toys in the Attic' is that it changes horses in midstream. It starts out as an inquiry into the moral consequences of wealth and ends up as a treatise on abnormal psychology. The more the focus narrows, the more the governing theme gets blurred" (*NY*, Mar. 5, 1960, p. 117).

In his comparison of *Toys in the Attic* and *The Three Sisters*, Jacob Adler regards the theme as the effects of money on human lives. Mr. Adler seizes perceptively on the nature of the form of the play, but perhaps misses the true theme. He calls *Toys in the Attic* "a fable about money, as startling, as artificial, as theatrical, and as true as *The Pardoner's Tale*. This is not merely an attempt at realism, which fails because of the artificiality. A fable does not have to apologize for artificiality. It is only necessary that it tell an interesting story, and tell it economically; that its characters display genuine human failings; and that the point it makes be universally true. . . . In *Toys in the Attic*, then, the genre is not problem play but fable, and the technique is not realism but what might be called realism stylized." [16]

Hellman strips her drama to the bone, employs not realism, but "realism stylized" to show the disastrous effects of having one's dreams come true when those dreams are false. In going beyond surface realism, Hellman for the first time observes the dramatic unities.

She observes them because she zeroes in on that one day only in the lives of her characters that is revelatory of the truth about their pasts and their irrevocable futures. What so permanently alters the lives of the Berniers is not the arrival of sudden wealth after a lifetime of poverty and penuriousness, nor is it the need to be loved. The basic theme about the human condition in *Toys in the Attic* reflects Hellman's constant, lifelong concern with the necessity for self-knowledge and the disastrous effects of its absence. Love and money are only the means effecting an end made inevitable by these characters' beginnings.

There is plenty of "love" in the play, but love is destructive when the giver and the recipient fail to understand its nature—and *their* natures. And money is destructive when it forces the characters out of their comfortable, familiar life-lies, lies begun in their childhood, their origins forgotten like toys in an attic, but still subconsciously directing their behavior. In the now-familiar terms of transactional analysis, the degree to which the child is in charge in each character determines his degree of self-perception.

Money is the catalyst that alters the chain of human relationships because it forces the sisters to face the truth. They have always told themselves and Julian that life would have been different had they had money. The money comes too late; it would have been too late at any time since their childhood. When Carrie and Julian ate on the back steps and Anna waited on them, it was already too late.

In order to show the harm wrought in the name of love by those who lack self-knowledge, Hellman once again uses the devices of irony witnessed in the earlier plays, with an ever-deepening skill. And once again her use of irony led critics to compare her to Chekhov. In "Miss Hellman's Two Sisters" Adler sought to demonstrate parallels in the Chekhov and Hellman plays with examples ranging from general parallels in plot and character development to rather dubious parallels in dialogue. He argued that "The basic similarity, and the basic difference, between the characters in *The Three Sisters* and *Toys in the Attic* is that, while in neither play do the characters want what they think they want, or ever get it, in *Toys in the Attic* they come to realize the truth and in *The Three Sisters* they do not" (p. 115).

Harold Clurman's account of the theme of the Hellman play is more accurate: "One's destiny is fashioned by what one does, and the dream of a goal other than that toward which one's habitual acts lead is mere self-deception" (*Nation*, Mar. 19, 1960, p. 261). This description certainly fits *The Autumn Garden* also, and one might regard *Toys in the Attic* as a fable told to make the closing line of *The Autumn Garden* absolutely clear: "Most of us lie to ourselves," says Constance. She might have then added, "Let me tell you a tale of two sisters who lived once upon a time in New Orleans."

In telling that tale, Hellman is once more an ironist. Again an arrival precipitates a change in the lives of the characters. Again there are characters who pass judgment on themselves. Much more obviously than in earlier plays, characters function as a chorus. Again the title is symbolic and there is no single protagonist. Although the movie version gave the audience a conclusive ending when Anna and Julian turned on Carrie, who was made the obvious villain of the piece, and left her virtually frothing at the mouth, in the play Hellman once again used an open ending. Julian still does not know at the end of the play who foiled his scheme. The audience, with its superior knowledge, knows that eventually he will find out and both sister and wife will lose him, causing Albertine Prine in turn to lose Henry. But the curtain comes down on the premonition, not the actuality. Again characters have self-explaining monologues. And again, with some of the finest lines Hellman has written, the dialogue differentiates the characters.

Like *The Autumn Garden, Toys in the Attic* is almost novelistic, containing descriptions of offstage events which could have been developed into full scenes. We are told about the way Julian and Lily lived in Chicago, about Julian's big scene with Warkins, and about the scene in Sailor's Alley when Julian and Mrs. Warkins are attacked and robbed by Warkins' thugs. And in addition we are given description of scenes from the past, important because they affect the present and are more real to Carrie, at least, than the actual present: Carrie and Julian eating on the back steps, Julian giving food to Gus, winning marbles from Gus and being forced to return them, Anna's eye operation, Julian's wedding.

In her attempt to go beyond the limits of the realistic form, to write a novelistic play, Hellman may have left the audience with at least one frustrating characterization—that of Albertine Prine. She emerges from nowhere to deliver judgmental remarks. She is basically a choral character, and we know less about her than we might expect for a character given such importance in the dialogue. We know that her grandmother once lived on the Berniers' street, that she has a lake house, that she loves a black man, and that she doesn't like Lily very much. This gives us little to go on, and yet we listen to her. Her words carry weight because they are ironic and seem to convey Hellman's ironic view of the other characters. And the principal virtue of *Toys in the Attic* is Hellman's use of irony.

In Carrie, she gives us a character who assumes a role when dealing with others. We discover also that Anna and Carrie have reversed roles, or, perhaps more accurately, that Carrie has created a role for Anna which she insists that Anna play. Albertine says to the two sisters, "Sometimes I can't tell which of you is speaking. (*To Carrie*) Your manner, Miss Carrie, is so, well, so Southern. And then, suddenly, you are saying what I had thought Miss Anna might say. It is as if you had exchanged faces, back and forth, forth and back." (Act I, p. 694) In a confrontation scene between Anna and Carrie we learn that Anna knows Carrie has made her acquaintances at the office think Anna controls Carrie's life.

Another kind of irony comes from characters who have insights other characters lack and thus speak ironically. Told that Julian has paid off the mortgage on the house, Carrie says, "Didn't he know we hated this house, always, always, always." Anna replies, "You used to tell him how much we liked it, and the garden, and the street, and the memories of Mama and Papa." When Carrie says, "You know very well I said all that to keep him from being ashamed of the house," Anna wryly says, handing her the canceled mortgage, "Well. We've been rewarded." (Act II, p. 708) Albertine says to Julian when he complains that no one is happy about the money: "There's something sad in not liking what you wanted when you get it. And something strange, maybe even mean. (*Sharply, as if in warning*) Nobody should have cried about your good fortune, nobody should have been anything but happy." (Act II, p. 722)

The sisters have self-revealing monologues. Anna says to Carrie: "I loved you and so whatever I knew didn't matter. You wanted to see yourself a way you never were. Maybe that's a game you let people play when you love them. Well, we had made something together, and the words would have stayed where they belonged as we waited for our brother to need us again. But our brother doesn't need us anymore, and so the poor house came down. . . . I am a woman who has no place to go, but I am going, and after a while I will ask myself why I took my mother's two children to be my own." (Act III, pp. 745–46)

Carrie tells Lily that she is afraid and explains what she is afraid of and for what reasons: "Of my hair which isn't nice anymore, of my job which isn't there anymore, of praying for small things and knowing just how small they are, of walking by a mirror when I didn't know it would be there— (*She gasps*) People say 'Those Bernier girls, so devoted. That Carrie was pretty, and then one day she wasn't; just an old maid, working for her brother.' They are right. An old maid with candied oranges as a right proper treat each Saturday night. We didn't see people anymore, I guess, because we were frightened of saying or hearing more than we could stand. (*Very angrily*) There are lives that are shut and should stay shut, you hear me, and people who should not talk about themselves, and that was us." (Act III, pp. 738–39)

Hellman employs "boomerang irony" in the plot. Again "the gods are just and of our pleasant vices make instruments to plague us." Had Albertine not had her strange relationship with Henry, Carrie could not have learned that Mrs. Warkins was black. Had Lily not made her nightworld trip to the Quarter when Julian couldn't have sex with her, Henry and Albertine might have been around to prevent Carrie's manipulation of Lily, instead of being off retrieving her ring. And so it goes.

The most traumatic boomerang is Julian's return with the money, forcing the recognition from all his women that they preferred him poor. Remembering Adler's comparison, one might speculate on the three sisters' reaction if their brother had announced that they were rich and could, at last and immediately, go to Moscow.

The fulfillment of Julian's boyhood dream brings Carrie's jealous, warped love into the open. When Julian comes, bringing the sisters what they always had told him they wanted, the child in Carrie surfaces, the child Anna had always known about. Albertine says, "I guess most of us make up things we want, don't get them, and get too old, or too lazy, to make up new ones. Best not to disturb that, Julian. People don't want other people to guess they never knew what they wanted in the first place."

Julian's success forces Carrie to face the truth that she preferred him dependent; his independence pushes her into almost open revelation of her true feelings for him. Anna sees, as she saw years ago. When Carrie says, "You used to tell us that when you love, truly love, you take your chances on being hated by speaking out the truth," Anna answers, "I'll take that chance now and tell you that you want to sleep with him and always have. Years ago I used to be frightened that you would try and I would watch you and suffer for you." (Act II, pp. 731–32) In the third act she tells Carrie, "You lusted and it showed. He doesn't know he saw it, but he did see it, and someday he'll know what he saw. (*With great violence*) You know the way that happens? You understand something, and don't know that you do, and forget about it. But one night years ago I woke up and knew what I had seen in you, had always seen. It will happen that way with him. It has begun." (Act III, p. 737)

Another element found in ironic drama, as we have seen, is the calm before the storm, the moment of false happiness before the catastrophe. In *Toys in the Attic*, not only is Julian's return with canceled mortgage, new clothes and furniture, and tickets to Europe a scene of false happiness in the usual ironic sense; we see the double irony that Julian is the only one made happy even at the moment: his women are dismayed. Julian is the agent of his own destruction. The gifts he brings, his new independence force the others to act to recreate the old order. Ironically, then, the scene that might close a traditional comedy—the prodigal ne'er-do-well returns a success and they all live happily ever after—is the beginning of the action in this play.

Julian's return, triggering the action, occurs late in the first act. Dashiell Hammett had complained when he read an early draft that Hellman had written half of the play and nothing had happened. Hellman wrote a "slow" first act because her real interest was in character revelation. That first act allows the audience to see the sisters' habitual acts, their daily routine, the "something," as Anna says, that they had made together. We see the habits of a lifetime: the weekly exchange of presents (always the same ones), the two sisters poring over "our travel book" (one thinks of James's "Four Meetings"). Carrie's speeches often begin with "you always" or "you used to." Threaded throughout are Carrie's constant references to Julian.

At thirty-four, he is still so close to his sisters that a two-week hiatus in letters alarms them. Two things hold the sisters' lives together in that shabby house that has grown as people left it: the (apparent) dream of going to Europe and Julian's (real) dependence on them. And how often that dependence has deferred the dream we know from Gus, the black iceman. "Where are you going this time?" he says.

Perhaps the most effective aspect of the Act I dialogue is its apparent discontinuity. Out of a lifetime of small talk made to cover the empty spaces in their lives, the two sisters have the habit of not answering directly. Hellman has perfected a device she attempted years before in *Days to Come*: "People in life, I told myself, don't always make the direct answer, or follow the immediately preceding thought" (*Six Plays*, p. ix).

In *Toys in the Attic* Hellman develops indirection to an art, as Carrie uses it to ignore what she doesn't want to face or to interpret people's words and actions to suit herself. Lily says, for instance, that she doesn't want money. Carrie says, "You mustn't worry about it. Not worth it." Lily protests that she isn't worried. Carrie, hearing what she wants to hear, answers, "I suppose rich people always worry about money." Lily again protests that she isn't worried about money. Carrie's final rejoinder is, "Well, you mustn't." (Act I, p. 699)

And so we come to know the Berniers with their lifelong struggle to stay middle-class. (The critics who called the house a "mansion" were wrong; the Berniers aren't faded aristocrats. They live in an ugly, shabby middle-class house that is growing shabbier with the years.)

Hellman's mastery of irony makes *Toys in the Attic* both character drama and dark comedy. She is interested in how the characters react when their bluffs are called about their dreams for the future. She had not been very interested in how the women would get the money away from Julian when she had discussed the play with Stern. "They loved him," she said, "for being the kind of Schlemiel that they brought him up to be, and they don't like the new independence. So they proceed to take the money away from him. I don't know the plot." When Stern asked whether that was what was holding her up, Hellman answered, "Partly. I'm making too much fuss about the plot, though. It's not really the plot, because the plot could go any way. It doesn't matter which" (*Contact*, p. 115). It didn't matter which because Hellman was interested not in what the characters did, but in why they did it. They fight to protect their false dreams, without which life would be meaningless.

Failure to change is a failure to grow. Julian is still a little boy, with a little boy's dreams of making his big sisters proud of him. Carrie, who has built her life around consoling Julian for his failures, can't cope with his sudden success. Anna, whose love for him is different, can. She can relinquish her dream of watching his children grow up, and go to Europe as he wants her to.

Their characters are delineated in the first act. They are clear to us. The rather perplexing characters are Lily and—as already remarked—Albertine, for different reasons. The character of Lily must be a real challenge to an actress. Is she retarded, disturbed, an innocent wanton? Occasionally her dialogue sounds like the dialogue Hellman gives herself as a young girl in the memoirs: "Because I must ask truth, and speak truth, and act truth, now and forever." Sometimes she sounds like Hellman's Joan of Arc remembering her moments of glory: "Did it rain? I don't remember. It was all days to me: Cold and hot days, fog and light, and I was on a high hill running down with the top of me, and flying with the left of me, and singing with the right of me—(*Softly*) I was doing everything nice anybody had ever done nice." (Act I, p. 699)

A reviewer called Albertine a character without a history. Along with Anna, she has the most literate, ironic, perceptive dialogue in the play. She seems to function primarily as a choral character, almost at times as a persona for Hellman: "But I have bad news for you, Julian—it's not simple being happy, and money doesn't seem to have much to do with it, although it has to do with other things more serious." The following speech of Albertine's contains a qualifier Hellman uses more than once in the memoirs (the italics are mine): "I am going to give you a good-bye present. Try to make use of it: the pure and the innocent often bring harm to themselves and those they love and, when they do, *for some reason that I do not know,* the injury is very great." (Act III, p. 747) Using another favorite Hellman phrase, "in space." Albertine says to Lily, who has just said she is sorry, "You have been saying you are sorry, in space, for many years," meaning without purpose or commitment. The scriptwriter for the movie version solved the problem of Albertine's characterization by cutting most of the character's lines and giving most of the remainder to other characters.

Like *The Little Foxes* and *The Autumn Garden, Toys in the Attic* acquires its unity of tone and its driving force from Hellman's view of the characters and the situation. As Sharpe says, the author of ironic drama gives us "a view of life, a mood, a psychological state . . . communicated from playwright . . . to audience," revealed through "the techniques used . . . to put the audience into that psychological state" (p. ix). In other words, once more we are given "fine distinction of mind" and "moral clarity."

In *Toys in the Attic* Hellman sets out to show us that we fool ourselves. All of us do: we must face that fact and attempt to rectify it, Hellman says. Those capable of understanding, who refuse to accept the truth about their motives and actions, harm not only themselves but those they claim to love. In this play money has been the catalyst, love has been the rationalization, but self-deception has been the driving force.

Although the play ends with a melodramatic beating and knifing, we don't respond as we would to melodrama because Hellman controls our attitude toward the characters with her detached treatment. John Gassner said of *Toys in the Attic*:

It is the special merit of Lillian Hellman's work that dreadful things are done by the onstage characters out of affectionate possessiveness, rather than out of ingrained villainy. Although the author's corresponding view of life is ironic and is trenchantly expressed, there is no gloating over human misery, no horror-mongering, no traffic with sensationalism in *Toys in the Attic*. And, unlike some well-known contemporary playwrights here and abroad, Miss Hellman has proved once more that she can deal with human failure without falling in love with it herself. She remains admirably sane in the midst of the ugliness and confusion she so unerringly exposes. [17]

Hellman distances us from the final scene because we have known about Lily's call to Warkins and because we are more interested in the effect of the beating on the other characters. Carrie is so happy that Julian says, "Why you start to purr at me?" Albertine knows that Carrie will tell Julian Lily telephoned Warkins and tells Carrie to let her know first so she can come for Lily. Henry has already said he won't be there if that day comes.

The curtain closes on Anna, who had been ready to make a definitive break with Carrie, picking up her valise to bring it back inside. Carrie has just bustled happily off to the store to get the ingredients for soup for Julian, who has "always liked" soup. Carrie's parting line is Scarlett O'Hara's—"Tomorrow's another day."

It is appropriate that Carrie has virtually the final word. She has exercised her will, and reality for her is what she wills it to be. Anna (and the critics) spoke of incest, but it is not that Freudianly simple. Carrie, in fact, wants something more, or other, than Julian as a lover. The germ of the character was in Hellman's Cora in *Days to Come*. Carrie wants to wake up and find that it is "years ago." She wants to be able to go back to the "secret place" with Julian, where the children got away from the grown-ups (reality). She wants to repeat all the rituals developed in childhood. Imagine a thirty-eight-year-old woman saying, "I can still jump. Shall I jump and you will catch me?" Carrie can't accept Julian's having sexual relations with any woman, perhaps not so much because she wants him for herself but because the act makes Julian a man, not a boy.

When Julian, changed less by the money than by his defiance of Warkins, seems to be departing forever from the romantic script Carrie has written for the two of them, she is driven to act; and in that action she changes from the aging, frustrated Southern belle she has appeared to be. It is as if Rose Griggs had become the child in *The Children's Hour*. Carrie is willing to destroy Julian-the-human-being to preserve her Julian-in-Never-never-land. As Charles Walcutt puts it:

> Here evil looks out of the frivolous void—strong, conscious, capable evil that plans and acts with shocking efficiency. By her frightful action Carrie defines and declares herself; she becomes responsible because she knows what she wants and plans how to get it, willing to hurt other people as much as is necessary to gain her end. . . .
>
> Clearly the plot provides Carrie's opportunity, and until it came she could not have known what she would do, could not therefore have known what she *was to become* by doing it. No amount of description or play of intellect could, I think, have made such wickedness even potentially real; it had to find itself in the act. It came into real being in the act. [18]

Alan Downer's insight into the characters of Carrie and Julian moves us once again to a view of Hellman the ironist, the writer of dark comedy:

It is not that, like the hero of *Death of a Salesman*, [Julian] had dreamed the wrong dream, that his values had been corrupted by a materialistic society. It is not that, like the heroes of whom Miller complains, he is the inadequate male who must yield to the all-powerful female. His life is shattered by a force unknown to the artist-sociologist or the artist-psychologist, by a force known only to the artist-moralist, the force of evil. Miss Hellman presents it directly and uncompromisingly. It is embodied in the younger sister, no capitalist dragon, no Satan lusting for revenge, no more incestuous than Ferdinand of *The Duchess of Malfi*. She is what evil must always be, the other side of good, tragic because she cannot know of her enslavement, because she can never have the opportunity to escape. She is the most memorable figure of a memorable work. [19]

To speak of *Toys in the Attic* in terms of incest, miscegenation, Southern decadence, is to miss the point. *Toys in the Attic* is a fable about what happens to adult children when their protective self-deception is stripped away. Carrie had warned Lily, "There are lives that are shut and should stay shut, you hear me, and people who should not talk about themselves, and that was us."

Carrie, as much a child as Lily, has made sure that Julian won't grow up; that Anna, who knows better, will be forced to go on playing Mother to the spoiled children; and that Mrs. Prine, who in a sense had sought her own escape from the sunlight of reality, must take responsibility for her strange daughter. And so they will live unhappily ever after.

CHAPTER 5

Nonfiction

There is no substitute for narrative sense, no matter how many different and entrancing charms may be set before us.

—Ezra Pound

I *War Pieces*

LILLIAN Hellman recently told an interviewer that she wrote plays because after *The Children's Hour* she was a playwright. She had written a few short stories and poems, but the success of her first produced play committed her to the theater. Through the years she said she would like to try a novel but she wrote no fiction. Had she not written the three memoirs, her reputation would rest solely on her theater work.

Between 1935 and 1969 Hellman wrote a few "occasional" nondramatic pieces, very few compared to the output of such playwrights as Tennessee Williams or Arthur Miller. These few dealt primarily with travel and with her visits to Spain during the Civil War and to Russia during World War II. Viewed chronologically, however, even these nonfiction pieces reveal a steady development toward the persona she used in the memoirs.

Out of her trip to Spain came an article for the *New Republic*, "Day in Spain," and several diary excerpts, collectively titled "The Little War," published in *This Is My Best*. The Spanish Civil War pieces are objective journalism, after Hemingway. Hellman's emphasis is on observed details rather than on her subjective reaction. Such emotional reactions as she reveals are made in direct statement: "I thought that these foreigners from everywhere were noble people. I had never used the word noble before, and it came hard, even to say it to myself. . . . Lying there, I prayed, for the first time in many years, that they would get what they wanted" (*NR*, Apr. 13, 1938, p. 298).

Even in describing her own reaction to shelling, Hellman uses

Hemingway's technique: the simple or compound sentence describing what she did, what she saw, rather than what she felt. With the exception of "A Blonde Lady" in *This Is My Best*, the Civil War pieces have the "careful," professional style of a war correspondent who only incidentally is a woman and a creative writer.

"A Blonde Lady" differs from the other pieces in revealing that Hellman has always been a masterful storyteller. The description of a harrowing drive through the Spanish countryside with a dangerously incompetent driver foreshadows the style of the memoirs. "A Blonde Lady" is swift-moving narrative, climaxed by a "scene" in which Hellman casts herself as the well-meaning foreigner finding her "party manners" inadequate to wartime experience.

The Kriendler Collection at Rutgers University contains an unpublished Spanish Civil War manuscript entitled "Richard Harding Davis, 1938." The article expresses strong antipathy toward a *New York Times* correspondent named Carney who avoids danger and is sympathetic to the Franco side. Since Hellman virtually calls him a fascist, it was probably too strong to be printed at the time.

Hellman's final war piece, "I Meet the Front-Line Russians," was published in *Collier's* in March 1945. Invited by the Russians and encouraged by our government to accept the invitation, Hellman visited Russia in 1944, a visit described in some detail in *An Unfinished Woman*. A comparison of the diary excerpts in that memoir with the published article reveals interesting differences.

The direct moral earnestness in Hellman's public utterances and writing outside the theater during the 1930s is admirable in the human being but less effective in the writing than the ironic tone she used in the plays. In a letter written from Paris in 1937 to E. B. White, James Thurber expressed his disagreement with the involvement of writers in the war: "It is the easiest thing in the world nowadays to become so socially conscious, so Spanish war stricken, that all sense of balance and values goes out of a person. Not long ago in Paris Lillian Hellman told me that she would give up writing if she could ameliorate the condition of the world, or of only a few people in it." [1]

Like Hellman's pieces on the Spanish Civil War, the *Collier's* article on Russia filters out her personality. The language is careful, the diction simple, the emphasis on factual detail. Perhaps a preference for one or the other is a matter of taste. If one compares the following excerpts, the first a diary entry in *An Unfinished*

Woman, the other from "I Meet the Front-Line Russians," one sees that the latter, while giving the same details, distances the reader with passive voice verbs and leaves Hellman, as camera eye, out of the scene. The diary entry uses the present tense and action verbs and involves Hellman and, consequently, the reader in the scene.

From the diary entry:

> I am sitting in a pine forest, propped against a tree. Not a sound can be heard, although there must be three thousand men spread out in the forest and a thousand horses, resting or being fed. It is a scene from another, long ago war, or the background for an opera. I put down my notebook to stroke the face of a horse who is pushing his nose into the snow and I am back in Pleasantville on another winter day, sitting in the snow, hot from the sun, patting the heads of a pony and a poodle. I want to be where I am. I want to stay in this forest (*UW*, p. 156).

From the *Collier's* piece:

> After an hour's drive we turned off the road and came suddenly into a wonderfully camouflaged clearing in the forest. Pine trees had been cut to make the clearing, and there were soldiers sitting on the tree stumps, smoking and cleaning their guns. Horses were tied to trees and looked beautiful standing there, pushing their noses into the snow. It was so quiet and calm that for a minute it seemed as if I must be in the pine clearing of my own farm; it was an old-fashioned scene as if from some other war, a long time ago (p. 68).

Neither the *Collier's* article nor diary excerpts record Hellman's visit to Maidanek, a concentration camp, shortly after it was taken from the Germans. Written for *An Unfinished Woman*, Hellman's reaction shows the mature writer using imagery to convey the emotional horror of the experience: "I was down in the blackness of deep water, pushed up to consciousness by monsters I could smell but not see, into a wildness of lions waiting to scrape my skin with their tongues, shoved down again, and up and down, covered with slime, pieces of me floating near my hands" (p. 153). Six months passed before she could bear to put the details of the experience in her diary. Writing twenty-four years later, she distances the details in a series of "that" clauses and says, "That morning, that afternoon, that what of time, did not have then, does not have now, any measure of hour-space or land-distance as I ever knew it before" (p. 153).

II   *Theater Pieces*

The *Collier's* article was the last of the war pieces, although her trip to Spain had influenced the content of her first article about her work, "Back of Those Foxes" (*NYT*, Feb. 26, 1939). In it she says that she thought about writing the play on her way out of Spain, to keep from thinking about the food she would soon be eating while people in Spain were starving. That statement may have caused reviewers to see *The Little Foxes* as a piece of social protest. "Back of Those Foxes" is well written but colorless, without the Hellman persona present in her later nonfiction.

Aside from the section in *Pentimento* called "Theatre," Hellman has written about her work only four times in her long career. In addition to "Back of Those Foxes," written in connection with the opening of *The Little Foxes* in 1939, she wrote "Author Jabs the Critic," a response to Brooks Atkinson's review of *Another Part of the Forest*; "Preface and Postscript," the introduction to *Four Plays* published first in the *New York Times*; and "The Time of the 'Foxes,' " a reminiscence of the first production, occasioned by the Lincoln Center revival of *The Little Foxes* in 1967.

In both "Author Jabs the Critic" and "Preface and Postscript" the style is polished and impersonal, even when Hellman recalls personal details. In the response to Brooks Atkinson Hellman defends her plays against the charge that they are melodramatic and "well-made."

In the introduction to *Four Plays*, as in all of these early pieces, the tone is still "public," that of a well-educated speaker addressing a group. Hellman again defends herself against the criticisms that her plays are melodramatic and well made. The mistake here lay in accepting the labels to begin with. In doing so, Hellman reinforced the labeling; and, since for years this introduction was the only written source of Hellman's view of her own work, writers were forever quoting her definitions of melodrama and well-madeness and attacking the definitions and defenses, rather than looking freshly at her work.

The war pieces are virtually free of metaphor. In the introduction to the plays Hellman begins to use a stylistic device she develops most effectively in the memoirs—the extended metaphor—as well as certain kinds of imagery she employs to a much greater degree later—"kinetic" images personifying the abstract: "It took a year and a half of stumbling stubbornness to do the play," the writer must "kick and fight his way through," "If he is good and drives ahead," "I played this theme all alone: a solitary composer with a not very interesting note."

Although critics seized on Hellman's remarks about melodrama and the well-made play, they ignored an idea that informs all her work: the necessity to do one's best. She says, "In any case, . . . this much has been right: I tried. I did the best I could do at the time each play was written. Within the limitations of my own mind and nature, my own understanding, my own knowledge, it was the best I could do with what I had. If I did not hope to grow, I would not hope to live" (*Six Plays*, p. xii). Critics, if they noticed these words at all, viewed them as apology rather than credo. When *Six Plays* was published in 1960, Hellman added: "I said then that I wanted to live to be a better writer. I still want just that. No need to write about it again" (*Six Plays*, p. xiv).

In 1967 Hellman wrote about the first production of *The Little Foxes*. She was also at work on what was to become *An Unfinished Woman*, and the style of this memoir is foreshadowed by the essay on *The Little Foxes*. She writes of the "strange memory that can lose years and people, but which can remember lines and rhythms written and heard in childhood." When she tried "to walk back through memory's lane," she "stumbled in the dark and lost [her] way." She says, "I see the trees of those days in clear sunshine but, although I know the forest must be only a very few feet away, I cannot seem to reach it" (*NYT*, Oct. 22, 1967).

She personifies the abstract: she had "sudden swings of anger," people believed in "the civil rights of something called temperament"; of the approach of World War II she says "the hurricane was somewhere off the coast, and death around the corner"; she dislikes "the aimless, spitball malice" of the time of McCarthy. She is already employing the device of "pentimento," seeing and seeing again, as in the essay she moves from the time of the foxes to the time of the blacklist, back to the Baltimore tryout, then to the time of revival. Then and now, vision and re-vision, and the then and now are one in the mind and the voice of the teller, the voice already that of the memoirs, personal, one talking to one, the voice of the familiar essayist, almost extinct in the days of modern journalism:

A few days after we opened in New York, I knew we were a success. Most certainly I wanted success; but most certainly I snarled at it. It took me years to find out that I was frightened of what it did to people and, instinctively, I did not trust myself to handle it. . . . But now, after "The Little Foxes," not even an isolated village in Cuba seemed to help. A time had come. I didn't know clearly what I meant, but I knew that my life had to change and change fast. I did not understand that 1939 was to be the holocaust year of our century but, like most people who had been in Spain during the Civil War and had seen something of Western Europe, I knew the hurricane was somewhere off the coast, and death around the corner (*NYT*, Oct. 22, 1967).

III *Political and Literary Articles*

For all her much-noted involvement in politics, Hellman wrote very few political pieces. In 1940 she wrote "The Little Men in Philadelphia," a piece on the Republican National Convention for *PM*. She realized, she says, that deals would be made and a candidate chosen; so she left a press conference and went to South Street, attempting to get political opinions from "little men," who proved afraid to talk.

In 1948 Hellman went to Yugoslavia to see a production of *The Little Foxes*. On the way she interviewed the vice-premier of Czechoslovakia and in Belgrade interviewed Prime Minister Tito. The *New York Star* published a series of articles about the trip. Hellman arrived during the epic Cominform disagreement.

Her first article presents an interesting mixture of her dislike of the German-American tourists on the plane, an encounter at Shannon airport with a drunk who insisted on buying her Grand Marnier at five in the morning, an explanation of the reason Dorothy Thompson and Rebecca West look more like literary figures than Hellman does (one doubts that her explanation endeared her to those two ladies), and the Yugoslav version of the Cominform attack. The second article is entirely devoted to an interview with Vice-Premier Fierlinger of Czechoslovakia, who explained Jan Masaryk's "suicide" and warned, "I would like to tell my capitalist friends that if they wish to maintain their way of life, they had better avoid war in Europe because they will wake up to find that the people of Europe won't fight for them" (Nov. 5, 1948). In the third article Hellman discusses *The Little Foxes* and European direction of American plays.

The next article deals entirely with the Tito interview, ending with a shrewd Hellman observation that proved to be correct: "I have a feeling it is simply a disagreement between two Socialist states and the rest of us have been naive in deciding that all Communists think alike, all the time, all their lives, as if they were robots and history were a stone monument waiting unchanged to allow all men to meet around her at the minute, in complete agreement" (Nov. 8, 1948). (Also another example of Hellman's use of metaphor to make the abstract concrete.)

In the fifth article Hellman tells the story of a former aristocrat and her family, who fought the Nazis during the war. The last of the series describes her memories of Paris at the time of the Spanish Civil War and ends with an airport conversation with movie czar Eric Johnston, who was gracious to her under the impression that she was Theresa Helburn. Of all the *Star* pieces, the one dealing with *The Little Foxes* is most like the later Hellman.

In 1963 Hellman attended the International Drama Conference in Edinburgh as an American delegate. In "Scotch on the Rocks," her short, highly sardonic critique, she says the conference bore out her theory that all theater people are actors manqué. Arthur Adamov became Shirley Temple, "although Shirley Temple was never so conscious of her charm." Wolf Mankowitz called Bernard Levin the "first Jewish fascist." "Mr. Mankowitz," says Hellman, "has had a sheltered life." Hellman uses her favorite metaphor to describe the theater: she writes of "that fashionable disease which caused the conference to come out in a rash—the need of the well-established to be anti-established, the belief that to question the work of the avant garde is to be square. Ibsen goes and Ionesco comes. Ionesco goes and Ibsen returns. . . . Fashion, as every society lady knows, takes a lot of doing and changes fast and the really expert practitioners of fashion never buy clothes in early September." Harold Clurman says Hellman managed to efface herself completely at the conference, proving her indomitability.

Two magazine articles, in 1963 and 1964, used the pole of memory to stir depths long buried, to borrow Hellman's borrowing from Henry James. In "Sophronia's Grandson Goes to Washington" Hellman uses as a central thread of the piece her search for Sophronia's grandson, who was supposed to be there. Inevitably, then, much of the piece deals with her memories of Sophronia as she wanders through the crowd waiting for Martin Luther King's speech.

The piece opens like a movie script, with Hellman propped against a marble column looking at the statue of Lincoln, waiting for Sophronia's grandson. "I realized again," she says, "how deep were my roots in the South, how I had loved it and not loved it, and how so much of me had been molded by a Negro woman, and molded to last for good" (*LHJ*, Dec., 1963, p. 78). Fade out, fade in. Quick narrative and description of Sophronia lead to a story of her father's rescuing a black girl from two rednecks on a station platform in Alabama. She ties this to a contemporary incident told her by some marchers and makes an accurate observation: "The Southern tightly held fantasy that the black man is, or can be, the enemy is no longer mild chatter among kindly white people whose grandfathers or great-grandfathers once owned slaves. What is called poor white trash came down among them with the industrialization of the South and, fastening on an ignorant and cruel belief, took action" (p. 80). The piece ends with an account of her meeting with a young black named George, who crops up again in the memoirs, anticlimactically bringing Sophronia's grandson to Hellman's house. The grandson, sullen and silent and hooked on heroin, doesn't remember Sophronia at all.

In "The Land That Holds the Legend of Our Lives," her 1964 visit to Jerusalem evokes memories of her childhood reaction to religious commitment as she listens to a Catholic priest. (The memoirs reveal that Hellman always was admiring-fearful of "committed" people, seeming not to realize that she herself was one of them. Perhaps she associated commitment with adherence to an external organization rather than to an ethical life-style.) Interestingly, though Hellman's sense of Jewishness is the core of this piece ("I sat for a long time . . . thinking that I was seeing the land that held the legend of my life—all that I believe and do not believe, the first words I ever heard, and, someday, the last I will hear"), the idioms are Southern: the roof was "mean with a searching wind," "I had better take myself along on home," "a mighty nice way of saying goodbye" (*LHJ*, April, 1964, pp. 57, 122).

In the 1920s Hellman had written some book reviews for the New York *Herald Tribune*, but only once in her career has she written an extended piece about another writer. In 1955 she edited *The Selected Letters of Anton Chekhov* for a series under the general editorship of her friend Louis Kronenberger. She may have accepted the assignment because of the financial difficulties of those blacklist years. She wrote a general introduction to the book and brief introductions to each section. She describes Russian intellectuals as "founder[ing] through the heavy seas they themselves had helped stir up, sometimes trying to meet new waves with a new twist of the body, sometimes deciding the waves had become too dangerous and it was time to make for shore."

In 1965 she also wrote a piece on Dashiell Hammett as an introduction to *The Big Knockover*, a collection of his stories— "Dashiell Hammett: A Memoir," first published in the *New York Review of Books*. With several concluding paragraphs added, it became the final section of *An Unfinished Woman*. Reaction to the Hammett recollection quite probably prompted the later book. Carlos Baker wrote, "The usual adjective is *moving*, which I certainly found it to be, but it was also thorough, beautifully written, funny, genuinely tragic, and wonderfully frank and loyal. It's by far the best writing in print about him, and makes a fine portrait-in-depth of a kind too rare in this or any other time" ("Letters," *NYRB*, March 6, 1966). The famous style of *An Unfinished Woman*, *Pentimento*, and *Scoundrel Time* is already there full-blown.

IV   *The Memoirs*: An Unfinished Woman

While *An Unfinished Woman* is a beautifully written book, fully deserving of the National Book Award and of its long run on the best-seller lists, it lacks the thematic unity of the later *Pentimento*, simply because, like Topsy, it "just growed." Hellman told an interviewer at the time that she was working on a collection of memory pieces, incorporating diary entries. The original intention seems to have been publication of something of an anthology of her Spanish Civil War and World War II experiences, together with the Hammett piece.

An Unfinished Woman furnishes tidbits for the "Docs and post-Docs," as Hellman calls researchers. They can, for instance, speculate about Hellman's mother as a possible source for Mother Hubbard in *Another Part of the Forest* or Lily in *Toys in the Attic*. They can note that the name for Nick Denery, the "meddler" in *The Autumn Garden*, may have come from James Denery the Third, a childhood playmate. They can supply factual details Hellman has no interest in. She says in *Pentimento*, "I no longer remember what year I went to Cuba for a vacation after the opening of what play and on my way to write what movie script," knowing full well that any number of Docs and post-Docs can supply that information. What they cannot supply is the spiritual, emotional, intellectual journey she embarks on in the memoirs, taking the reader on many fascinating side trips, but never losing sight of the destination.

Simply by writing these books she may have precluded what she fears: would-be unauthorized biographies. She has given readers the meat and left bare bones for the academics. One can legitimately examine the memoirs, however, as examples of her craftsmanship and as evidence of the further growth of a writer.

The structure of *An Unfinished Woman* is roughly chronological. Within that structure Hellman begins to employ the treatment of time which results in the seamless unity of *Pentimento*. The short first chapter, for instance, begins conventionally enough—"I was born in New Orleans to Julia Newhouse"—but within it the reader is given a quick sketch of Hellman's great-uncle Jake, "witty and rather worldly, seeing his own financial machinations as natural not only to his but to the country's benefit, and seeing that as comic"; a sketch of her mother, "lifelong lonely for the black men and women who had taught her the only religion she ever knew," complete with illustrative anecdote, and direct self-analysis of the problems of an only child.

The central image of chapter two is a fig tree which Hellman makes the reader see with concrete detail. Hellman says she learned there, fishing from the tree in gutter water, that anything in water "was of enormous excitement" to her, and a thread of imagery running through all the memoirs confirms it.

A Hellman self-analysis is apt to follow a "then-later-now" sequence: "it was in the fig tree, *a few years later*, that I was first puzzled by the conflict which *would haunt* me, harm me, and benefit me *the rest of my life*. . . . I *already guessed* . . . although . . . I pretended *for the rest of my life*" (italics mine).

The reader is introduced to Hellman's "rampage anger" in brilliant narration of a runaway from home climaxed by her first menstrual period. A lasting image is of Hellman asleep in a backyard doll's house, complete with child-sized furniture, evoking a picture of Alice in the white rabbit's house. The section ends with an insight Hellman gained from the experience, a piece of knowledge all lifelong rebels seem to know: "if you are willing to take the punishment, you are halfway through the battle."

The overall structure remains straight-moving narrative, with a chapter devoted to her time at NYU, one to the Liveright days, then Kober and Hollywood, but within these chapters she moves ahead to Hammett and one glimpses untold potential short stories given in parentheses or a throw-away clause: "a few years after that he killed

himself and a male companion in a Zurich hotel room," "Her father
was a rich Jew from Detroit and she was already started on the road
to Marxism that would lead her, as a student doctor, to be killed in
the Vienna riots of 1934." (Reading the memoirs, one is struck by
how few Hellman acquaintances die in bed.) All this dropped in an
offhand manner in the midst of a very funny story of Hellman and
friends explaining "flaming youth" to Samuel Adams.

Within the introduction to an account of her 1937 trip to Europe
comes an explanation of her feelings about the theater, developed at
more length in *Pentimento*, an explanation also illustrating her
"time-binding" with the sequence of tenses: "I *know* as little *as I
knew* then about the conflict that *would keep* me hard at work in a
world *that is* not my world, although it *has been* my life" (italics
mine).

On her way to Moscow she stopped in Paris, where she met the
Beautiful People of the 1920s, Gerald and Sara Murphy of *Living
Well Is the Best Revenge* and Fitzgerald's *Tender Is the Night*, and
saw Hemingway again. (The reader meets Hemingway three times
in the book; and, although Hellman protested, truthfully, that she
didn't set out to portray him unflatteringly, the simple truth of the
anecdotes depicts him as the Writer as Ugly American.)

The mid-section of the book opens abruptly with diary entries
from her trip to Spain. The entries for October 14 and 20 prove to
be part of the article "Day in Spain." The October 22 entry is
essentially "A Blonde Lady." Still another entry tells of an evening
with Hemingway, who first thinks Hellman a coward when she
refuses to go out on a balcony with him to watch the shelling, then,
when she insists on driving through the bombs to keep a radio
commitment, tells her she has " '*cojones* after all.' "

Coming out of a war brings you, Hellman says, "face to face with
what will happen to you after death." In London, faced with
frivolous dinner conversation, she describes her reaction in a series
of verb phrases qualified by other verb phrases, an effective stylistic
trait running throughout the memoirs and another way of bringing
to bear what was to be and had been on what was: "I thought, My
life, all I felt in Spain, is going out in drip-drops, in nonsense, and I
suddenly was in the kind of rampage anger that I have known all my
life, still know, and certainly in those days was not able, perhaps did
not wish, to control." The rampage is climaxed by a broken ankle,
the first of many twisted ankles that accompany Hellman's moments
of anger.

She takes the reader from London, to the Pleasantville farm, to 52nd Street, where "a woman who was never to be committed was facing a man who already was." Hammett wins one of the many arguments he won with Hellman by pronouncing an ultimatum, walking down the sidewalk away from her, challenging her to let him go. He wins, of course, just as he does another day by putting a cigarette out on his cheek to stop her complaints. (These incidents appall some feminists.)

An attempt to summarize the narrative of her Russian trip in 1944 would lead to Byzantine convolutions, as one gets a mixture of 1944, 1967, and years in between, Hellman writing herself into the organization—the vision, rather—of *Pentimento*, for the two are one. (To refresh her memory, she made two trips to Russia in the late '60s while researching for *An Unfinished Woman*.) Introducing the reader to the diary sections, Hellman says that, when she "read them again last year, and again last week, they did not include what had been most important to [her], or what the passing years have made important."

Hellman uses here a time device used again in *Pentimento*, a device as old as Laurence Sterne's *Tristram Shandy*. Work written to be read cannot by the nature of the medium have the immediacy of drama, which happens "now," before one's eyes. Narration throws even this morning's newspaper into the past. Hellman achieves dramatic immediacy by making the time of the writing the reader's present: "And there are many entries about Sergei Eisenstein and our almost daily cup of tea, but I didn't know, couldn't know, that twenty-one years after his death he is more real than many of the people I saw last week." Of a three-year-old Russian orphan she visited weekly she says, "I couldn't know then that I would think about him for years afterwards, and dream as recently as last month that I was riding with him on a toboggan." In *Pentimento* one reads "Yesterday, nineteen years later, standing in . . . a cemetery at Edmund Wilson's funeral, I thought of Henry Sigerist and knew why" (*P*, p. 192).

The Russian diary entries contain the material published in revised form in "I Meet the Front-Line Russians." One learns, in a passage withheld in 1945, that Hellman had a chance to go into Warsaw with the Russian army, turned it down, "not in fear for [her] life, but in fear of [her] nature." In this passage and many others in all three memoirs, Hellman speaks of her "nature," and the nature of other people. She uses the word in what today seems to be an old-fashioned sense, as a description of traits formed early in life, stable and, consequently, knowable. Today, when one's "nature" sometimes seems to be regarded as adaptable to the fashion of the moment, like one's hair style, and when people as otherwise disparate as Charles Colson and Charles Manson "find God," it may be refreshing rather than limiting to think that one can count on one's "nature."

Of the visit to Russia in 1966, Hellman writes of memories of the past stirred by the trip, of the first night in Moscow when she shut herself in a hotel room with cigarettes and vodka to hunt down a period of her life she had "thrown . . . somewhere, always intending to call for it again, but now that it came time to call, [she] couldn't remember where [she] had left it." In one of her extended metaphors, she wonders if other people "drop the past in a used car lot" and leave it there until they can't "even remember the name of the road."

For her, she says, "The road had to be to the lake in Pleasantville. But at first, I could only remember the last day I had ever walked it." She lives through that moment in her life, then files it away as something that can never come again "because [she] could never again be that woman." She returns to the 1966 diary and to the caricaturist always present in Hellman. In the charges and counter-charges made by America and Russia Hellman sees "the moral tone of giants with swollen heads, fat fingers pressed over the atom bomb, staring at each other across the forests of the world" and finds that vision comic.

Anything and everything in Russia remind her of something from her personal past. She refuses to count the rubles in royalties given her, wonders if her "dislike of counting money could have started at [her] grandmother's Sunday dinners where they spoke of things in exact dollar amounts," says she cares so much about money that she has always "pretended not to care." Hellman writes of this ambivalence more than once. Being a poor relation of "the little foxes" caused in her "a wild extravagance mixed with respect for money and those who have it."

Captain K, whom she had met in 1944, asks her to explain William Faulkner's *Sanctuary* and evokes memories of the South that anticipate *Pentimento*: "the South I knew, full of vines and elephant ear leaves, heavy with swamp air and Spanish moss, home and frightening land." This memory leads to a Faulkner anecdote, to memories of 1944 rehearsals of her plays, to a shrewd evaluation of Norman Mailer.

Another section of *An Unfinished Woman*, like the last section of *Pentimento*, is about a black woman she loved. Both end with Hellman in Cambridge. The section in the earlier book, while titled "Helen," is just as much about Sophronia. Hellman opens the section with a lyric passage on how she has always loved the water and what lives in it. The description flows into an extended metaphor, itself leading into her feelings about Helen and Sophronia. Again we see Hellman's time-binding: "One night about six months ago . . . it occurred to me that these childish, aimless pleasures . . . might have something to do with the digging about that occasionally happens when I am asleep. It is then that I awake, feeling that my head is made of sand and that a pole has just been pulled from it with the end of the pole carrying a card on which there is an answer to a long-forgotten problem, clearly solved and set out as if it had been arranged for me on a night table" (*UW*, pp. 229–30).

"On that night" Hellman was awakened by a crash downstairs, found a ceiling light-fixture smashed on the floor: "as I stood looking at the pieces on the floor, I thought: Of course, one has been dead three years this month, one has been dead for over thirty, but they were one person to you, these two black women you loved more than you ever loved any other women, Sophronia from childhood, Helen so many years later, and it was all there for you to know two months ago when, poking about the beach, a long distance from the house Helen and I had lived in, I found a mangled watch, wondered where I had seen it, and knew a few hours later that it was the watch I had bought in the Zurich airport and that had disappeared a short time after I gave it to Helen" (*UW*, p. 230).

That Faulknerian sentence weaves many threads of time together: the time of the writing, a night six months before, three years before that night, thirty years before that night, two months before the time of the writing, and the time of the watch-buying.

Hellman begins the next Faulknerian paragraph with "From the night of that rainstorm in Cambridge, for weeks later, and even now, once in a while, I have dreamed of Sophronia and Helen, waking up sometimes so pleased that I try to go on with a dream that denies their death, at other times saddened by the dream because it seems a deep time-warning of my own age and death" (*UW*, p. 231).

The paragraph is an example of skillful handling of sentence rhythm: after several long sentences, the last a series of long predicates, the penultimate sentence is a shorter question, the last sentence short, monosyllabic, declarative: "Why had these two women come together as one for me? Sophronia had not been like that." Memories of Helen lead to memories of Sophronia and Hammett (Helen was numbered among the many people Hammett didn't like). Hellman is as emotionally open in this section as it is perhaps possible for "her nature" to be: "Oh, Sophronia, it's you I want back always. It's by you I still so often measure, guess, transmute, translate and act. What strange process made a little girl strain so hard to hear the few words that ever came, made the image of you, true or false, last a lifetime?"

The last section of *An Unfinished Woman* is the Hammett piece. It begins in the middle of things: "For years we made jokes about the day I would write about him." In this beautifully written piece, both eulogy and elegy, Hellman never says she loved, loves Hammett, but gives a description of deep and sustained emotion that is definitive. To the Hammett piece as originally printed Hellman added the much-quoted, now-famous lines: "But I am not yet old enough to like the past better than the present, although there are nights when I have a passing sadness for the unnecessary pains, the self-made foolishness that was, is, and will be. I do regret that I have spent too much of my life trying to find what I called 'truth,' trying to find what I called 'sense.' I never knew what I meant by truth, never made the sense I hoped for. All I mean is that I left too much of me unfinished because I wasted too much time. However."

Reviewer response to *An Unfinished Woman* was almost exuberant. Joseph Epstein said, correctly, that the book is not "strictly a memoir. It is instead an attempt, and a rather severe attempt at that, at self-examination" and made an apt comparison: "There is something of the quality of a very superior American movie of the thirties about *An Unfinished Woman*. It is the work of a woman at once knowing yet without cynicism, tough yet generous, honest yet reticent—a female and super-literate Humphrey Bogart" (*NR*, July 26, 1969, p. 27).

Critics praised the style and found the style an extension of the character of the woman. Dorothy Rabinowitz said, "The quality of her experience has been extraordinary and that is no accident. It is an inevitability of spirit, that which creates experience. It is that which creats her language, too. Her speech is not poetic; it is stark and abrupt, but the force of its observation makes this conscientiously plain-speaking sensibility move as it does. . . . But it is more than style: it is the deepest of feeling, coming plain and meant to be that, enlarged nonetheless by its clarity and infectious in its precision." Rabinowitz compared the style of the memoir to the style of the plays: "Miss Hellman's dramaturgical instincts permit no conversation, no word, no twitch of a face, no walk across a room which does not create a scene. No silence is permitted which does not make a speech, no gesture which does not add to the creation; the scenes come with a striking power that for me, at least, never was there in Miss Hellman's plays" (*Commentary*, Dec., 1969, p. 95).

Robert Kotlowitz, calling *An Unfinished Woman* a "lucid, flinty, vulnerable book (in which the compressed prose is diamond-hard and sometimes brilliant and the dialogue is like one pithy speech after another out of a Hellman play)," said, "It is how many of Lillian Hellman's plays end, the plots neatly tied up and easily comprehended, while an uneasy sense of the future and its ironic dependence upon the past lurks just beyond the final curtain" (*Harper's*, June, 1969, pp. 92, 87). Such critics as V. S. Pritchett were taken with the persona, with the "terrific energy, . . . combative spirit and sudden charm," with the "ironic giving of the truth and quick taking back, the cool movement to the edge of revelation, then the urbane withdrawal." Terrific energy, combative spirit, sudden charm, qualified by the ironic, the cool, the urbane tone and style—add sardonic humor, and one has the viewpoint and attitude of the plays.

By the time of *An Unfinished Woman*, Hellman had moved from the impersonal, public tone of the early nonfiction to "dramatic" organization, with Hellman herself as the protagonist and viewpoint character. She had mastered the use of sentence and paragraph rhythm to create a mood, convey an attitude. She had developed fully the use of extended metaphor, of the concrete to convey the abstract. She had always kept her plays free of the "poetic," of figures of speech, believing that they stuck out like "Christmas tree ornaments." She had learned by the time of *An Unfinished Woman* that such metaphors could become organic to the written prose, could advance the action like dialogue by making idea and feeling concrete. There remained only the freeing of the structure chronologically, removing the necessity for writing around the diary entries. The techniques, the way of seeing were there. Hellman had mastered in the independent sections of the first memoir the techniques of organizing memory and self-analysis in time-whorls around a central figure or image: Helen, a fig tree, a watch half-buried in the sand. In *Pentimento* she was to demonstrate the complete mastery of the method as vision gave technique, technique revealed vision.

V *The Memoirs:* Pentimento

Pentimento, the book with the title few readers had heard of but none would forget, in 1973 occupied the best-seller lists for more than four months and received even stronger critical praise than *An Unfinished Woman*. The surface structure of *Pentimento* is roughly chronological; the underlying structure is spiral: each section is built concentrically around a central symbol, with the tension gradually rising to the sections "Julia" and "Theatre," then slowly subsiding to "Pentimento."

The memoir is subtitled "A Book of Portraits" and Hellman explains the term "pentimento" in an epigraph, an explanation that also reveals the structure of the book: "seeing and then seeing again." Critics were struck by Hellman's narrative power; one reviewer suggested *Pentimento* as required reading for would-be writers who wanted to learn how to tell a story. Hellman brings to the memoir the devices of twentieth-century fiction, together with the techniques of drama. Perhaps the most important device is the flashback, shaped to Hellman's particular purpose. In *Pentimento* the flashback is both a journey back in time and a journey into the self.

An Unfinished Woman opens in an apparently traditional manner: "I was born to Julia Newhouse." *Pentimento* begins like a modern short story, in the middle of things: "The letter said, says now." Hellman immediately gives the reader two times, the past tense of narrative, the present of drama. Although technically everything Hellman narrates is in the past, the narration may move to the future in relation to the time of the incident narrated, then move back into the past in relation to the original incident, then to the time of the writing itself, often culminating in "I was never to know," "I was never to find out."

The first section revolves around a woman and an object: Bethe, a cousin who unintentionally taught Hellman the power of love, and a valise containing family journals and letters. The reader winds up as frustrated as Hellman by the vanishing valise, having to make do, as in a detective story, with hints, clues, and indirections. Around the figure of Bethe, the reader is given the story of Bethe's arrival in New Orleans, Hellman's childhood memories, glimpses of Bethe through the passage of years, the time of *The Children's Hour*. With the reader's, and Hellman's, last glimpse of Bethe one is in the time of Hammett, and Hellman says to Bethe, " 'It was you who did it. I would not have found it [love] without you. Now what good is it, tell me that?' "

Hellman handles narrative summary in a novelistic fashion: "From the time I was fourteen until I was twenty-five, I had no news of Bethe . . . . I thought of her as I got dressed for my wedding . . . . Then I don't believe I ever thought of her again through a pleasant marriage that was not to last, until the first afternoon I slept with Dashiell Hammett."

In a summarized conversation with Bethe, Hellman introduces narrative threads picked up later in the book: "my beloved friend Julia . . . , my mother's Uncle Jake and his money, and how bad it was to live without my old nurse Sophronia." And, of course, to the reader of *An Unfinished Woman* Uncle Jake and Sophronia evoke memories of one's own.

Hellman gives a typical "punch" ending to an anecdote: "When it was all over, Styrie was found clinging to a fire escape with his right hand because his left hand was lying on the ground."

"Bethe," like the book as a whole, has many extended metaphors: "(God help all children as they move into a time of life they do not understand and must struggle through with precepts they have picked from the garbage cans of older people, clinging with the passion of the lost to odds and ends that will mess them up for all time, or hating the trash so much they will waste their future on the hatred.)"

The reader is given an example of the "tough" Hellman: a policeman laughs at her and "with that laugh cause[s] a lifelong, often out-of-control hatred of cops, in all circumstances, in all countries," and the self-mocking Hellman: "I was at my high-class moral theory stage, from which I have never completely emerged, and I had even had time to learn that it often worked."

The closing vignette, with its jungle imagery, is out of a Rousseau painting. (Hellman consistently uses imagery of roots, vines, tangled woods.)

The second section, "Willy," also begins *in medias res*: "He was married to my ridiculous great-aunt." Around the larger-than-life figure of Willy cluster other larger-than-life figures, some almost grotesque, as if written by Faulkner out of Dickens with Fitzgerald's moral imagination. We get not only Willy then, later, and now, but Aunt Lily, the too-thin lady with the morphine habit, and her black lover-pusher chauffeur; Caroline and Flo Ducky, Sophronia's aunt and niece; a night in Cajun swamp country; and the machinations of United Fruit (now United Brands) in the banana republics.

The complications of the narrative times in this section are not readily summarized—they move from *Toys in the Attic* to Hellman's childhood, from the time of Hollywood, to her adolescence, to the time of the writing. A striking example of a Hellman story-in-a-sentence is a glimpse of Honey, Aunt Lily's mentally-retarded, sexually-advanced son. The reader learns that Honey eventually was "put away" for several rapes and would-be rapes and died in a "looney bin." At one point in the narrative Honey, child-man excited by thoughts of his mother's relationship with the chauffeur, pins Hellman to a wall and attempts to insert his " 'thingy.' " " 'Open up,' he shouted into his future. 'Open up.' "

The section contains some of Hellman's most telling self-analyses. Another look at and dismissal of her attitude toward money: "to protect what little I had to protect I constructed the damaging combination that was not to leave me until I myself made money: I rebelled against my mother's family [the little foxes], and thus all people who were rich, but I was frightened and impressed by them; and the more frightened and impressed I grew the more aimless became my anger. . . . By fourteen my heart was with the poor except on the days when it was with those who ground them under. I remember that period as a hell of self-dislike, but I do not now mean to make fun of it: not too many years later, although old shriveled leaves remain on the stump to this day, I understood that I lived under an economic system of increasing impurity and injustice for which I, and all those like me, pay with ridiculous wounds to the spirit."

As she does in any piece dealing with her girlhood, Hellman quotes her father extensively in this section. Though Hellman generalizes more than once about her mother's character and personality, she never analyzes her father. Instead, he makes the kind of put-down remark to wife, sisters, and daughter, part-gibe, part-banter, that Hellman later puts in Hammett's mouth, although Mr. Hellman's talk is more gayly affectionate, less "tough" than Hammett's.

In an account of her incomplete and unconsummated weekend in the bayou country with Willy, one finds swift narrative, insistent concrete description, and analysis and description of love. The section is more compelling than a somewhat similar section in Walker Percy's novel *The Moviegoer*. In a swamp of cypress, swamp oak, fern, "wild high dark green leaves," and "flat small things the shape of salamanders," the young girl knows desire for Willy and wild jealousy, and runs away: "There are many ways of falling in love and one seldom is more interesting or valid than another unless, of course, one of them lasts so long that it becomes something else, like your arm or leg about which you neither judge nor protest. I was not ever to fall in love very often, but certainly this was the first time and I would like to think that I learned from it. But the mixture of ecstasy as it clashed with criticism of myself and the man was to be repeated all my life."

The next section, "Julia," is the private emotional apex of the book as "Theatre" is the public apex. Hellman retells the journey to Moscow via Paris she had told in *An Unfinished Woman* with Julia's story omitted. A comparison of similar sections in both books reveals a difference in tone. That of *An Unfinished Woman* is leisurely; the beginning of "Julia" is compressed, quick, intense.

Hellman's narrative organization is like a movie script. A phone call from Julia sets the narrative in motion. The phone call sends Hellman to a rendezvous at the railroad station which she almost muffs out of nervousness, then to a train compartment where she finds a hat box and a box of candy with unclear instructions attached. She knows one of the two boxes contains fifty thousand dollars and, numbed with indecision, Hellman sits as . . . fade out, fade in, flashback to the first night Hellman, twelve years old, was allowed to spend the night at Julia's grandparents' house: "Now, so many years later, I could climb the steps without a light." It was New Year's Eve, says Hellman, and "Each New Year's Eve of my life has brought back the memory of that night."

Hellman summarizes both personal and world history, interspersing concrete anecdotes, vignettes of time spent with Julia: a camping trip, a visit to Oxford, a sailing vacation, gifts exchanged through the years, then only occasional letters and cards as Hellman and Julia go down different roads which converge as the world approaches the holocaust years. Hellman gives us one more concrete scene, in Vienna after the bombing of the Karl Marx Hof, when Hellman sees Julia briefly in a hospital, doesn't realize her leg has been amputated. At Julia's order Hellman returns to America,

later hears from her that she has a daughter, named for Hellman. . . fade out, fade in to the train compartment on the way to
Berlin in 1937.

Hellman and Julia meet briefly between trains in a restaurant
where Hellman gives her the hat with fifty thousand dollars of Julia's
money in the lining to be used to free political prisoners. Hellman
wants to stay but Julia tells her it's too dangerous and sends her
away, promising to bring the baby to her in New York. But they
were never to meet again. After that Berlin meeting only a few brief
postcards, then a wire informing her of Julia's death in London.
Julia's family is indifferent, and Hellman flies to London, brings
Julia's knife-slashed body home, tries to find Julia's baby, is
prevented by the outbreak of the war. Hellman has Julia's body
"cremated and the ashes are still where they were that day so long
ago." Julia's courage and commitment live in both *Pentimento* and
Watch on the Rhine.

Reviewers had complained that Hellman said nothing of her
theater career in *An Unfinished Woman*. Hellman comments briefly
in *Pentimento* on each play chronologically. Within that chronology
she again takes the reader on concentric journeys into the past and
into her feelings about the theater and events and people she
associates with the time period of each play. The section is titled
"Theatre," as if "theatre" were another Hellman character. "The
manuscript," she says, "the words on the page, was what you started
with and what you have left. . . . the pages are the only wall against
which to throw the future or measure the past." She compares her
instinct for the theater to her instinct for boats and water. Instinct
has its reasons which reason cannot know.

Memories of *The Children's Hour* involve a quarrel between her
mother and father as to whether she was the "sweetest-smelling
baby in New Orleans," a meeting with a bemused Lee Shubert, and
the drunken opening night, including an effectively written party
scene in her hotel suite.

Days to Come leads her to her feelings about failure, particularly
in the theater. Her screenwriting days bring a funny story of
Hellman and a fellow writer's spending days trying to roll and stuff
condoms into match boxes with a writer friend's picture on the
covers. Hellman gives the impression that the time was as well
spent as any she spent in Hollywood.

Hellman devotes the most space to *The Little Foxes*, to the
difficulty of the writing and her dependence on Hammett, to the
difficulty of the casting and Tallulah Bankhead's bizarre behavior

offstage, to tryout days in Baltimore. With Tallulah dead, Hellman can retell the story of "The Time of the 'Foxes' " and have the last word.

The reception of *The Little Foxes* leads to an analysis of theater criticism and her bewilderment at the response to the play. Audiences and critics had misunderstood the Hubbards. In *Pentimento* Hellman attempts to explain them in terms of her mother's family, particularly her mother's uncle, Jake.

A Hellman extended metaphor sums up the writing of *Watch on the Rhine*: It "came out in one piece, as if I had seen a landscape and never altered the trees or the seasons of their colors. All other work for me had been fragmented, hunting in an open field with shot from several guns, following the course but unable to see clearly, recovering the shot hands full, then hands empty from stumbling and spilling."

Hellman rapidly covers the remaining plays: *The Searching Wind, Another Part of the Forest, Montserrat, The Autumn Garden* (with more memories of Hammett and "the best time of [their] life together"), *The Lark, Candide*, the writer's block that followed; finally, *Toys in the Attic* and a Hammett anecdote that ties then with now. With the failure of *My Mother, My Father and Me* Hellman leaves the theater, the finality felt in the sentence rhythm: "For most people in the theatre whatever happens is worth it for the fun, the excitement, the possible rewards. It was once that way for me and maybe it will be again. But I don't think so."

The section "Arthur W. A. Cowan" was first published in *Esquire* as "A Man of Unnecessary Things," the title taken from Hellman's description of Cowan. The section begins in the middle of an evening with Theodore Roethke, capering drunk. In the course of the evening one meets in passing Robert Lowell and Babette Deutsch. Hellman, without apparently realizing it, is a walking encyclopedia of American literature, having known personally every writer of any significance from Gertrude Stein to William Styron. (Styron, incidentally, dedicated *The Confessions of Nat Turner* to Hellman.)

The Cowan section contains more dialogue than any other, perhaps because, as Hellman says, she remembers more about him than she does about most people, perhaps to give the flavor of a man Hammett called "a crazy man . . . pretending that he [was] crazy." For an impatient woman, Hellman was quite patient with Cowan's theatrics and childishness for a number of years.

The narrative takes the reader to a party Cowan gave in

Hellman's honor, climaxed by an argument on the way home that causes her to leave his car in the middle of the Pennsylvania turnpike. This incident stirs thoughts about Cowan—thoughts reminiscent of *The Autumn Garden*: "I was what he wanted to want, did not want, could not ever want, and that must have put an end to an old dream about the kind of life that he would never have because he didn't really want it. We have all done that about somebody, or place, or work, and it's a sad day when you find out that it's not accident or time or fortune but just yourself that kept things from you."

Some years later there is a final maniacal diatribe from Cowan and Hellman sums him up in an extended metaphor: "I knew something had gone wrong with Arthur, now forever: the inside lines that hold most of us together had slackened or broken and bad trouble was ahead . . . . [All of his life], certainly much I didn't know about, had made the life into a line on a fishing reel that tangled and couldn't be untangled, held by a hand that didn't have the sense or the courage to cut the line and tie it together in another place. But I had to cut the line of me where it crossed and tangled with his, and that night I did it."

Cowan dies not long after, his death as befogged and mysterious as his life, and, as Hellman says, "He has disappeared." Before his death Hellman could no longer "pay him the compliment of anger," but in *Pentimento* she gives him what he perhaps might most want—a permanent niche in the annals of a remarkable woman.

The word "turtle" would be enigmatic enough in itself as title for the next section of *Pentimento*, but Hellman encloses it in quotation marks. Do they mean "this is a turtle essay"? Or do they mean "Maybe I was wrong and this name then is apocryphal," as scholars put quotation marks around the name "Longinus"? Or do they mean "This is not about a turtle at all"?

Hellman begins the section with a prologue, a swift narrative of a day in 1965 when she almost drowned off Martha's Vineyard. Finally carried against a piling by the same capricious current that had almost swept her out to sea, Hellman remembers another time, another day: "Holding to the piling, I was having a conversation with a man who had been dead five years about a turtle who had been dead for twenty-six." The reader is then plunged into the middle of things once again, with a verbal "long-shot" of the Pleasantville farm; then Hellman pans in to a close-up of the daily and seasonal activities through the years there, all ended by the

McCarthy period. "The time of doing what [she] liked was over in 1952."

The camera pans in again to the day Hellman remembers best, the day "Turtle" crippled Hammett's favorite dog. The day Hammett sets the traps, they catch the, not *a*, but *the* turtle. Hammett kills the turtle but it refuses to die, causing trouble between Hammett and Hellman. It is almost as if the turtle's tenacity forces a confrontation between two different philosophies of life. Hellman finally calls the New York Zoological Society for an authoritative statement as to whether the turtle is dead or alive and gets an unauthoritative answer: " 'You asked me for a scientific opinion. . . . I am not qualified to give you a theological one. Thank you for calling.' "

Hellman stubbornly refuses to make soup of the turtle, decides to bury it in spite of Hammett's ragging. (One critic otherwise delighted by *Pentimento* felt Hellman too often set herself up as wide-eyed straight man for Hammett's one-line wisecracks. Perhaps such criticism is not germane, but it does cross one's mind.)

The tone of the end is ironic understatement. Hammett wins again. Hellman buries the turtle inadequately, animals dig it up, Hammett reburies it, complete with wooden tombstone reading " 'My first turtle is buried here. Miss Religious L. H. ' " Camera moves from close-up of tombstone to long shot and fade out.

The title piece of *Pentimento* is the epilogue. Hellman is in Cambridge again, this time right after Hammett's death. Helen, Hellman's cook, makes friends with a college boy, who becomes a friend of Hellman's. Jimsie may be in the story to show the reader life goes on. He may be there to speak the curtain line. Many nights, unable to sleep, Hellman goes to stare at the nursing home where Hammett would have stayed had he lived. Helen, worried and angry, attempts to talk to her about death:

"You go stand in front of that place because you think you can bring him back. Maybe he don't want to come back, and maybe you don't—" she shrugged, always a sign that she had caught herself at something she considered unwise or useless to continue with.

It was a long time before I knew what she had been about to say.

Later on that spring, just before she leaves Cambridge, Hellman wakes from a dream and once more goes to stand vigil. Jimsie appears, sent by Helen. Hellman says "Pentimento," doesn't answer Jimsie's question about the meaning.

Helen dies; Jimsie takes the body home to South Carolina. The last few pages summarize the years Hellman has known Jimsie. "Everybody else in this book is dead." The book ends with a conversation with Jimsie:

"He said, 'I loved Helen.'

" 'Too bad you never told her so. Too late now.'

" 'I told it to her,' he said, 'the night I looked up your word, pentimento.' " Curtain.

With the publication of *Pentimento* the critical rockets went off. Some excellent students of American literature led the way— Richard Poirier and the late Mark Schorer. Poirier made a comment particularly applicable to "Turtle": "The inference to be drawn is that Hammett challenged precisely the kinds of submerged continuity, the marvelous inner sense of connectedness, the ability to bring disparate things together which is the special genius of this book, with its subtle yet intensely clarified grasp of possible analogies between quite different places, different people and different times" (*Washington Post*, Sept. 16, 1973).

Critics once again compared the nonfiction and the plays. "The dramatic quality is everywhere evident . . . in the author's exquisite sense of timing, a kind of poised power over the units of scene that few writers of fiction possess. But there is also the extraordinary gift for the precise detail, which is a fictional quality, and then again, for the often comically explicit detail," said Mark Schorer, who went on to describe Hellman's prose as "prose as brilliantly finished as any that we have in these years" (*NYTBR*, Sept. 23, 1973, pp. 1, 2). Richard Poirier said that "*Pentimento* provides one of those rare instances when the moral value of a book is wholly inextricable from its immense literary worth, where the excitations, the pacing, and the intensifications offered by the style manage to create in us perceptions about human character that have all but disappeared from contemporary writing" (*Washington Post*, Sept. 16, 1973). "It is the force of original vision that keeps the portraits true, their drama tense and present," wrote Dorothy Rabinowitz (*World*, Aug. 28, 1973, p. 39).

Again one finds in the critical articles phrases like "beauty and the power" and "poised power." Hellman had harnessed that immense power that, in her own words, "nearly blew a stage to pieces," had encased it in a style that had both the force and the precision of a laser beam. What she did in sections of *An Unfinished Woman* she perfected in the whole of *Pentimento*. The emotional structure, the line of development, are as clean and as sure, both in the separate parts and in the whole, as that of a "well-made" play.

The ear for the rhythms of the American-English sentence can't be taught; Hellman had developed that ear early in her dramatic career. She is a novelist born who has written novelistic plays and now has brought that fictional gift to the memoir, creating works of nonfiction as organically shaped and formed as a good twentieth-century novel. In addition to her sense of prose rhythm and her gift for the precise, the necessary detail, Hellman brings a mastery of the interweaving of time necessary to the memoir as *pentimento*, a term which fits all three books. That mastery includes the "layering" of verbs and predicates to qualify one another and link together disparate segments of time. Her flashbacks deftly and unobtrusively perform the same function as the inner monologue or stream-of-consciousness in the novel or the self-revealing monologue in a Hellman play. In both *An Unfinished Woman* and *Pentimento* Hellman's most important journeys are inner, not outer ones.

The sum of *Pentimento* is more than that of the portraits that are its parts, for it gives the reader a portrait of a lady who, while judging others, reserves the severest judgments for herself, whose clarity of mind and moral sensibility make readers question themselves, perhaps the best gift a book can give in these times.

VI *The Memoirs:* Scoundrel Time

Neither *An Unfinished Woman* nor *Pentimento* deals with the McCarthy period. Hellman had given her reasons, in *Pentimento* and in interviews, for not writing about the period. But in 1976 she finally wrote what she knew, what she saw, what she suffered. *Scoundrel Time* focuses on a limited period in the national madness that began in the late 1940s and subsided in the late 1950s (or took other forms). Hellman points out the connections between the "witchhunt" days, Vietnam, and Watergate and doubts our ability to remember long enough to avoid doing it all over again: "It is not true that when the bell tolls it tolls for thee: if it were true we could not have elected, so few years later, Richard Nixon. . . . And one year after a presidential scandal of a magnitude still unknown, we have almost forgotten them [the Nixon scoundrels], too. We are a people who do not want to keep much of the past in our heads. It is considered unhealthy in America to remember mistakes, neurotic to think about them, psychotic to dwell upon them."

Scoundrel Time is a frustratingly slim volume, made thicker by an introduction by Garry Wills (author of *Nixon Agonistes*) which gives the background of the McCarthy Inquisition for those too young or too forgetful to remember it. Hellman's memoir could have stood alone. What she gives the reader is a personal, moral history.

Scoundrel Time is different from the other two memoirs. Hellman will not let anything deflect the straight, strong narrative drive, what one critic called the "understated fury." If *An Unfinished Woman* and *Pentimento* were portraits in oil, *Scoundrel Time* is a black-and-white engraving. Gone are the "interior flashbacks." Gone are the extended metaphors that had become almost a trademark of the style. The few metaphors do not describe deep emotion but diminish the subjects described: "It was not the first time in history that the confusions of honest people were picked up in space by cheap baddies who, hearing a few bars of popular notes, made them into an opera of public disorder, staged and sung, as much of the congressional testimony shows, in the wards of an insane asylum." (In all three memoirs Hellman uses diminutives pejoratively: kiddies, baddies.) "Nor had we been surprised or angered by Cohn and Schine playing with the law as if it were a batch of fudge they enjoyed after the pleasure of their nightly pillow fight." McCarthy, Cohn, and Schine were, she says, "indeed, a threesome: . . . Bonnie, Bonnie and Clyde, shooting at anything that came to hand on the King's horses that rode to battle in official bulletproof armor."

She tells of her dinner with Clifford Odets and his table-pounding bravery, followed by his naming names; her drink with Elia Kazan, followed by *his* naming names and publishing an apologia in the *New York Times*. Kazan's fears for his movie future lead to the story of the Hollywood producers' Waldorf meeting and Hellman's refusal to sign the loyalty oath thenceforward demanded of screen people.

Never one to mince words, Hellman calls Nixon a "villainous liar," as she recalls news photos of him holding up the microfilms found in the famous pumpkin in the Hiss case. "Facts are facts," she continues, pointing out what any kid who makes a jack-o'-lantern knows—a hollowed-out pumpkin deteriorates. "If facts are facts, and should not be altered, then which of us, as individuals or in groups, did the alterations and why?" A rhetorical question not answered here. She asks, in a modern American paraphrase of Voltaire, "Since when do you have to agree with people to defend them from injustice?"

She takes the reader back to the spring of her testimony with "That was a tough spring, 1952." The Internal Revenue Service was investigating both Hellman and Hammett. Joseph Rauh, Hellman's attorney, had discovered, as does everyone who researches Hellman's plays, that the *Daily Worker* had criticized *Watch on the Rhine* as a war-mongering play, coming as it did while the Nazi-Soviet Non-Aggression Pact was still in effect. The *Daily Worker* had also been critical of Hellman's favorable remarks about Tito during his difficulties with the Cominform in 1948. Hellman refused to use this defense: "in my thin morality book it is plain not cricket to clear yourself by jumping on people who are themselves in trouble." Hellman's insistence on observing the spirit, not the letter of the law must have been a sore trial to the legal people.

Hellman gives the text of her justly famous letter to the House Un-American Activities Committee and excerpts from a diary of the time, showing her very human fears. She puzzles over Clifford Odets's behavior: "It is impossible to think that a grown man, intelligent, doesn't have some sense of how he will act under pressure. It's all been decided so long ago, when you are very young, all mixed up with your childhood's definition of pride or dignity." In his piece on *Scoundrel Time*, Murray Kempton objected to this judgment, arguing that one's adult ethics don't spring from family Sunday dinners. But this is Hellman's story and, for her, at least, and for many people, it *was* decided a long time ago. William Faulkner evidently agreed, in writing "That Evening Sun," a story in which Jason Compson the child foreshadows what he will grow up to be. One remembers the lines quoted in Graham Greene's "The Basement Room": "In the lost childhood of Judas Christ was betrayed." (Kempton himself makes essentially the same point as Hellman in his *Part of Our Time*.)

The next and longest section takes the reader from the time of the hearing to the day Hellman left the farm. One sees Hellman on her way to the hearing, with the sense to be afraid and the character to act with courage, anyway. It is difficult to write a scene about oneself as heroine but Hellman does it by ironic undercutting, as she does in her plays. She doesn't understand the legal sparring, annoys the committee counsel by saying "I must" when he wants "I do."

As Hellman's future as a writer hangs in the balance, she hears one little old lady say to another, "Irma, take your good cough drops." But it is another overheard voice that makes the difference.

After the committee has made the tactical error of inserting Hellman's letter in the record, Rauh distributes copies to the press in the back of the room. As the reporters read the statement, Hellman hears, "Thank God somebody finally had the guts to do it," and she says, "I still think that unknown voice made the words that helped to save me."

She goes back to the farm, puts it up for sale. She and Hammett agree not to break up the land, even though she could get more money for the lots. Hellman undercuts even this decision by adding, "a fine sentiment with which I agree and have forever regretted listening to."

Hellman had been scheduled to read the narration for a concert performance of Blitzstein's *Regina*. She wanted to cancel after the hearing, feeling sure the audience would be hostile. Blitzstein wouldn't let her. Hellman remembers best about that night a nameless, red-headed stagehand who gave her a couple of shots of bourbon before she went on. If one has become involved in the book, the diary entry for that evening is quite moving, partly because of the straightforward narration, partly because of the style, the switch in tenses to convey otherwise unstated emotion: "I got halfway across the stage, staring straight ahead, saying something to myself, some prayer, I don't remember. Suddenly there is thunderous applause. It is so unexpected that I stop dead center in such shocked surprise that the first few rows began to laugh. Then the audience rose, applauding, and I face it, unable to move. For a second I think that the applause is meant for the musicians, but they have risen too, and Marc tells me later that I looked behind me to see if the applause was meant for somebody else." Hellman undercuts this scene by giving the stagehand the last word. He motions her off the stage, gives her a ginger ale bottle full of bourbon and tells her to carry it back on stage with her.

If this were a Hollywood movie, the story could end here, quoting, perhaps, Hellman's final words about the sale of the farm and the animals: "I knew that day I would never have any of them again. But whenever I said that to myself I also said that I was lucky ever to have had them at all, and that is what I feel today, these many years later . . . . I am angry that corrupt and unjust men made me sell the only place that was ever right for me, but that doesn't have much to do with anything anymore, because there have been other places and they do fine."

But it is all-too-real life, and Hellman moves swiftly through the years of the blacklist. She is hired for little (and bilked of part of that) to do a movie adaptation she would not have touched had she had money, is spied on by CIA informants, sees her income dwindle to little or nothing, takes a part-time job in a New York department store under an assumed name. The surviving aunt in New Orleans dies, leaving her enough money to last until the success of *Toys in the Attic*, and during the last year of Hammett's life she no longer has to worry about money.

In a short epilogue Hellman tells the reader she is still angry at the people who let McCarthyism happen. She blames McCarthy, Richard Nixon, and the rest of the boys in the band less than the liberals who did nothing to stop them. One thinks again of *The Little Foxes*: "Well, there are people who eat the earth and eat all the people on it like in the Bible with the locusts. Then there are people who stand around and watch them eat it. Sometimes I think it ain't right to stand and watch them do it."

The coda is quintessential Hellman in style and content: "I have written here that I have recovered. I mean it only in a worldly sense because I do not believe in recovery. The past, with its pleasures, its rewards, its foolishness, its punishments, is there for each of us forever, and it should be.

"As I finish writing about this unpleasant part of my life, I tell myself that was then, and there is now, and the years between then and now, and the then and now are one."

It is true of all three memoirs, but particularly of *Scoundrel Time*, that one cannot measure the book without taking measure of the woman, a fact the critics recognized. The *Time* reviewer called her "a polished stylist and an invaluable American" (May 10, 1976, p. 83). (Kempton was bothered by *Time*'s reversal toward Hellman. Since Henry Luce's death, however, *Time* sometimes has a kind word for liberals, even for a few Democrats.) *Newsweek* called the tone of the book "laconic, reserved, unfooled— . . . as distinct as Orwell's" and summed up with: "This book about an 'unpleasant part of my life' leaves us exhilarated. The only truth Hellman doesn't tell—maybe she's shy about this—is what a terrific life she's had" (Apr. 26, 1976, p. 96).

In the *National Observer* (May 1, 1976, p. 19), *Scoundrel Time* was praised because it, "for all its moral vigor, does not carry the weight of a sermon; and the reason is Hellman's own remarkable style. She puts down words on paper the way a woman talks who is sure enough of her own judgment to let its oddities show." Praising

the "sassy point-blank grace" of all three memoirs, the reviewer
concluded that the "intensely personal" quality of the book is both
its "literary value" and its "moral strength": "It is a great lady's
refusal to compromise herself for personal profit, a private record of
a terrible time."

Geoffrey Wolff, writing of all three books, said, "Put in moral
terms, the proper execution of these books is a demonstration of
Miss Hellman's good character; put in sentimental terms, they
make a happy ending to as much of Miss Hellman's story as she is
ready to tell." He ends with a judgment of the woman: "She has
lived by a code grounded in courage. She is quick, by her own
account, to respond to injustice, and despises cruelty with a force
that can itself be cruel. She will not be fiddled with, or place her life
in hostage to little people of little care for it. In London she left a
dinner party, kicking over her chair, because people asked her
offhand questions about the Spanish Civil War, from which she had
just come. . . . Well, she put a stop to that, and now we have these
books, a mighty force of life, a rush monitored, hot and cold mixed
with exquisite calculation" (*New Times*, Apr. 30, 1976, pp. 64, 65).

Pulitzer-Prize-winner Robert Coles called her then and maybe
now "a lonely figure—brave precisely because she was afraid, and
knew the power and cunning of her accusers." He was moved to
think of Kierkegaard, who would, he believed, "have loved
Scoundrel Time for its fine, sardonic humor, its unsparing social
observation and, not least, the skill of its narration. . . . He longed
for companions who would summon personal memory, among other
modes of expression, to the task of making concrete and specific
ethical analyses—as opposed to cleverly worded abstractions that
conceal as much as they tell. In Lillian Hellman he has a kindred
spirit, and we a voice making itself heard in what still is, alas, a
wilderness of bluff, guile, and deceit" (*Washington Post*, May 9,
1976).

Novelist Maureen Howard, comparing playwright with memoir-
ist, said that "memory has become a liberation: as she speaks
directly to us her voice, unshared with her characters, has a new
freedom. For a mind like Hellman's the imagination is enlarged not
limited by the facts of her life. She has forged a remarkable
autobiographical style which relates the emotionally charged
moment to a wide cultural reference." Miss Howard invoked the
name of Camus: "Her self-reliance is extraordinary: in her
insistence on writing her story 'then and now' she has, in Camus's

terms, dedicated herself to the duration of her life. She has not been content with the success of the past but has gone on to a new career, and in writing her memoirs she remains responsible for everything that happens to her" (*NYTBR*, Apr. 25, 1976, p. 2).

The political Right responded predictably. Hellman's old friend Diana Trilling was so unpleasant in *her* memoir that Little, Brown refused to publish the book. William F. Buckley, apoplectic at Hellman's receiving an invitation to present an award at the 1977 Academy Award ceremonies, compared Hellman to Nazi Albert Speer and titled his review of *Scoundrel Time* "Who Is the Ugliest of Them All?" Old-Left-New-Right Sidney Hook also attacked Hellman in *Encounter*, and Alfred Kazin conducted an intra-Jewish quarrel in *Esquire*.

In a piece as much personal response as review, Murray Kempton disagreed with much of Hellman's assessment of the period but concluded: "It was enough for Miss Hellman to have done the single great thing of having once and for all defined the issue." Quoting "I am not willing to bring bad trouble to people," Kempton added, "Rather that I endure my own. That is all that seems finally important about the way she did what she did, and it is a great deal. It would be too much to credit it with any more tangible historical result. The Committee went on just as it had." One must disagree with Kempton here. Hellman made judgment possible by behaving as she did. Her behavior simply showed such behavior to be possible and probably made it easier for Arthur Miller to take such stand as he did take. (Some people, including Lillian Hellman, are not as admiring of Miller's testimony as Kempton.)

Speaking of Hellman's sense of honor, Kempton writes, "You feel here the operations of a genuine nobility and no small part of a shrewd instinct about the future, an awareness—and such senses have much to do with honor—of how the thing would look in due course." Due course might not have arrived in Hellman's lifetime. Some creative people died; others lived while their talent died. Hellman risked all rather than have the "wounded name" Miller has so often written about. She could not then know the answer to the question she once put to Hammett about being a survivor. Kempton continued with reservations about the pleasures of having Hellman for a comrade, but concluded, "The most important thing is never to forget that here is someone who knew how to act when there was nothing harder on earth than knowing how to act" (*NYRB*, June 10, 1976, pp. 22-25).

Never to forget, always to remember. Because of these books and the life revealed in these books, Hellman speaks to us with great moral authority. In 1975 she was asked to deliver the commencement address at Barnard College. She reviewed for the graduates the loss of individuality and individual freedom, the corruption in public life, the time of the scoundrels, and ended: "I came here today—I don't like to make speeches—to say that I think it is your duty to put an end to all that. Your absolute duty" (*Mademoiselle*, Aug., 1975, p. 167).

It was certainly not the best of times, it was perhaps the worst of times, it was a time of scoundrels and sad clowns, it was a time when one cranky Southern-Jewish lady risked her material and creative future for simple human decency, shaming those who would do less. One remembers Hellman's gentle mother talking to the rednecks threatening a black girl in the darkness of a Southern depot platform, "You boys had better take yourselves along on home."

CHAPTER 6

An Ironic Vision

THE moment of summing up arrives; yet, if summing up suggests finality, one cannot make final judgments. As rare as it may be in American letters (Scott Fitzgerald said there are no second acts in American lives), Hellman, in her seventies, is in full career.

Although *The Collected Plays*, which Hellman regards as the definitive edition of her theater work, was published in 1972, no important critic has reevaluated her work. Jacob Adler, a specialist in Southern writers, published his Hellman monograph in 1969 before the publication of the collected plays and the memoirs. Richard Moody's book, *Lillian Hellman: Playwright*, published in 1972, contains no original criticism. Doris V. Falk's *Lillian Hellman* (1978) is primarily biography based on interviews and the memoirs.

A generation of theater-goers and theater students have been conditioned to associate the name Hellman with the terms "well-made play," "melodrama," "social protest." If this cultural reflex persists, then Hellman's metaphor of fashion in the theater will continue to describe her critical reputation.

An unnecessary stumbling block to a fresh perception of Hellman is the "political" label. Although, as Jacob Adler comments, "to one assessing her as an artist, politics—particularly her political problems in the Fifties—seems almost entirely beside the point," [1] political partisanship is not likely to subside in the foreseeable future.

The Hellman vision is nonetheless moral, not political. Robert Corrigan and John Gassner arrived independently at the same judgment: Gassner said, "Miss Hellman concerns herself generally with damnation as a state of the soul, and a case might be made out for saying that her real theme, whether she knew it or not, is 'original sin' in a modern context, which brings her closer to such contemporary Catholic writers as Mauriac than to Bernard Shaw or Karl Marx." [2] Corrigan concluded that "she cannot be considered, as she so often is, a social writer; rather, she is interested in showing damnation as a state of the soul, a condition that cannot be reformed out of existence or dissolved by sentimentality or easy optimism." [3]

Murray Kempton said that Hellman's behavior before the House committee was partly determined by her sense of how things would look in due course. For "in due course" substitute the "days to come" of the Old Testament, days determined by human actions today. Engagement, commitment, self-knowledge, and self-acknowledgment of responsibility are the virtues Hellman urges on her audiences and readers. If the memoirs had never been written, the moral vision is clear in play after play.

As critics of the memoirs have pointed out, Hellman's moral vision is inseparable from the ironic vision and voice. Though obviously more overt in the memoirs, the voice is there in the plays. And, "[a]s soon as an ironic voice has been used to any extent in any work of any kind," says Wayne Booth, "readers inevitably begin to take interest and pleasure in that voice—in the tasks it assigns and the qualities it provides; it thus becomes part of whatever is seen as the controlling context." [4]

In *The Context and Craft of Drama*, James Rosenberg raises a pertinent question: "why must generic classification necessarily degenerate into a game of hierarchies? Is it not enough to perceive that there are various modes of perception . . .?" What we should recognize is "a way of seeing, not a trick of writing." [5]

Any final judgment must include a perception of Hellman as ironist, with a way of seeing, and seeing again. This is not to say that such an awareness will necessarily cause a reader to prefer Hellman to other major American playwrights. But it should prevent one's judging her by inapplicable criteria. To "rank" Hellman in a Williams-Miller-Odets-whoever list is, as she might put it, "a losing game." In the modern American theater Lillian Hellman is *sui generis*, and a careful reading of her plays reveals that those generally considered her best (*The Little Foxes*, *The Autumn Garden*, *Toys in the Attic*—to which list might be added *Watch on the Rhine* and *Another Part of the Forest*) are the most fully ironic (and novelistic). By the same criteria, *Pentimento*, in which Hellman most completely employs fictional techniques and a controlling ironic voice, is the superior memoir.

D. C. Muecke has described irony as "intellectual rather than musical, nearer to the mind than to the senses, reflective and self-conscious rather than lyrical and self-absorbed," having the qualities of "fine prose rather than . . . lyric poetry." [6] Readers and audiences with no predilection for irony will perhaps prefer Arthur Miller's pathos of the common man, or perhaps Tennessee Williams' poetry of the sensitive, bruised soul. There will always be those, however, who will turn to Lillian Hellman for a view of life trenchantly expressed, often moving, frequently funny, uncomfortably accurate in its ironic vision of the fools met in the forest—and the fools *those* fools meet. In judging Lillian Hellman's work, critics might abandon the automatic genre labeling and examine her way of seeing and her appraisal of things seen, remembering that there is more than one valid way of looking at a blackbird. And a writer.

Notes and References

Chapter One

1. Morris Gelman, "A Theatre Portrait: Lillian Hellman," *The Theatre*, June, 1960, p. 15.
2. Tallulah Bankhead, *Tallulah* (New York, 1952), pp. 237–44.
3. Harold Clurman, *All People Are Famous* (New York, 1974), p. 160.
4. Stefan Kanfer, *A Journal of the Plague Years* (New York, 1973), p. 83.
5. *Minority Report* (New York, 1963), p. 430.
6. *Hearings Before the Committee on Un-American Activities, Eighty-Second Congress, Second Session, May 19, 20, and 21, 1952*, "Communist Infiltration of the Hollywood Motion-Picture Industry—Part 8," p. 3545.
7. Eric Bentley, ed., *Thirty Years of Treason: Excerpts from Hearings before the House Committee on Un-American Activities, 1938–1968* (New York, 1971), pp. 532-33.
8. *Fanfare* (New York, 1957), p. 172.
9. Margaret Case Harriman, "Miss Lily of New Orleans," *Take Them Up Tenderly* (New York, 1944), p. 97.
10. Otis L. Guernsey, Jr., ed., *Playwrights, Lyricists, Composers on Theater* (New York, 1974), pp. 26–27.
11. *People*, November 24, 1975, pp. 18–20.
12. *Rolling Stone*, February 24, 1977, p.54.
13. *Family Circle*, April, 1976, p. 27.

Chapter Two

1. *Theory and Technique of Playwriting* (New York, 1949), pp. 264, 266.
2. *New Theatre and Film*, March, 1937, p. 15.
3. *Lillian Hellman: Playwright* (New York, 1972), pp. 56–57.
4. "A Critical Analysis of the Plays of Lillian Hellman" (unpublished Ph.D. dissertation, Yale University, 1961), pp. 83, 84.
5. *Robert Benchley: His Life and Good Times* (Garden City, N.Y., 1970), p. 179.
6. *The Best Plays of 1934–35* (New York, 1935), p. 33.
7. "Lillian Hellman's Indignation," *The Dramatic Event* (New York, 1954), p. 75.

8. Alan S. Downer, ed., *American Drama and Its Critics* (Chicago, 1965), p. 199.

9. *The Theatre in Our Times* (New York, 1954) p. 406.

10. "Introduction," *Six Plays* (New York, 1960), pp. viii–ix.

11. Richard Hayes, *Commonweal*, January 16, 1953, p. 377.

12. Richard Stern, "Lillian Hellman on Her Plays," *Contact* 3, i (1959), 118–19.

13. *Stage*, April 1, 1939, p. 55.

14. *American Dramatic Literature* (New York, 1961), pp. 88–89.

15. *Theatre World*, February, 1946, p. 20.

16. *American Writing in the Twentieth Century* (Cambridge, Mass., 1960), p. 96.

17. John Gassner, ed., *A Treasury of the Theatre: From Henrik Ibsen To Eugene Ionesco* (New York, 1964), p. 984.

18. *Irony in the Drama: An Essay on Impersonation, Shock and Catharsis* (Chapel Hill, N.C., 1959), p. 48.

19. *A Theater in Your Head* (New York, 1967), p. 246.

20. *The Theatre in Our Times*, p. 370.

21. *The Political Stage: American Drama and Theater of the Great Depression* (New York, 1974), p. 401.

Chapter Three

1. *Theatre Arts*, March, 1947, p. 57.

2. *"The Searching Wind* in the Making," *Quarterly Journal of Speech*, 31 (Feb., 1945), 27–28.

3. Bagtry's wish to go to Brazil is an example of the result of Hellman's justly famous research. The descendants of unreconstructed Rebels still live in Americana, Brazil, attend a white-frame Protestant church, eat biscuits and gravy for breakfast, and speak English flavored with a soft Southern drawl and a tinge of Portuguese.

4. *Explicator* 24 (Oct., 1965), Item 20.

5. *In Search of Theater* (New York, 1953), p. 9.

6. *The Theatre in Our Times*, p. 370.

Chapter Four

1. *Fifty Years of American Drama: 1900–1950* (New York, 1951), p. 140.

2. *Of Irony: Especially in Drama* (Toronto, 1967), p. 92.

3. *Anton Chekhov* (New York, 1972), p. 76.

4. Lillian Hellman, ed., *The Selected Letters of Anton Chekhov* (New York, 1965), pp. xxiv, xxv.

5. Ibid., p. xiii.

6. Ibid., p. 5.

7. *Masters of the Drama* (New York, 1954), p. 737.

8. *Theatre at the Crossroads: Plays and Playwrights of the Mid-Century American Stage* (New York, 1960), p. 136.

9. *Fifty Years of American Drama*, pp. 140–41.

10. "*The Autumn Garden*: Mechanics and Dialectics," *Modern Drama* 3 (Sept., 1960), 191–95.

11. *Lillian Hellman* (Austin, Tex., 1969), pp. 33-34.

12. Lee Strasberg, ed., *Famous American Plays of the 1950s* (New York, 1962), pp. 18–19.

13. "Lillian Hellman on Her Plays," *Contact* 3, i (1959), 114.

14. Ibid., p. 116.

15. *The Reporter*, March 31, 1960, p. 43.

16. "Miss Hellman's Two Sisters," *Educational Theatre Journal*, 15 (May, 1963), p. 115.

17. *Dramatic Soundings: Evaluations and Retractions Culled from 30 Years of Dramatic Criticism* (New York, 1968), p. 483.

18. *Man's Changing Mask: Modes of Characterization in Fiction* (Minneapolis, 1966), p. 31.

19. *Recent American Drama* (Minneapolis, 1961), pp. 41-42.

Chapter Five

1. Burton Bernstein, *Thurber* (New York, 1976), p. 384. (Biographer Bernstein is Leonard Bernstein's brother.)

Chapter Six

1. Jacob Adler, *Lillian Hellman*, p. 14.

2. *A Treasury of the Theatre*, p. 984.

3. *The Modern Theatre* (New York, 1964), p. 1074.

4. *A Rhetoric of Irony* (Chicago, 1974), p. 176.

5. *The Context and Craft of Drama* (Scranton, Pa., 1964), p. 172.

6. *The Compass of Irony* (London, 1969), p. 6.

Selected Bibliography

PRIMARY SOURCES

1. Plays

Another Part of the Forest. New York: Viking, 1947. Reprinted: New York: Viking, 1962; with *The Little Foxes*, New York: Penguin, 1977.

The Autumn Garden. Boston: Little, Brown, 1951.

Candide: A Comic Operetta Based on Voltaire's Satire. New York: Random House, 1957. Reprinted: New York: Avon, 1970.

The Children's Hour. New York: Alfred A. Knopf, 1934. Reprinted: New York: New American Library, 1962.

Days to Come. New York: Alfred A. Knopf, 1936.

The Lark. Adapted from the French of Jean Anouilh. New York: Random House, 1956.

The Little Foxes. New York: Random House, 1939. Reprinted: New York: Viking, 1961; with *Another Part of the Forest*, New York: Penguin, 1977.

Montserrat. Adapted from the French of Emmanuel Roblès. New York: Dramatists Play Service, 1950.

My Mother, My Father and Me. New York: Random House, 1963.

The North Star: A Motion Picture about Some Russian People. New York: Viking, 1943. (film script)

The Searching Wind. New York: Viking, 1944.

Toys in the Attic. New York: Random House, 1960.

Watch on the Rhine. New York: Random House, 1941. Also limited edition of 349 copies, privately published, New York: 1942. Reprinted: Cleveland: World Publishing Company, 1943.

2. Collections of Plays

The Collected Plays. Boston: Little, Brown, 1972.

Four Plays. (*The Children's Hour, Days to Come, The Little Foxes, Watch on the Rhine*) New York: Modern Library, 1942.

Six Plays. (*The Children's Hour, Days to Come, The Little Foxes, Watch on the Rhine, Another Part of the Forest, The Autumn Garden*) New York: Modern Library, 1960.

3. Memoirs

Pentimento: A Book of Portraits. Boston: Little, Brown, 1973. Reprinted: New York: New American Library, 1974.

Scoundrel Time. Boston: Little, Brown, 1976. Reprinted: New York: Bantam Books, 1977.

An Unfinished Woman: A Memoir. Boston: Little, Brown, 1969. Reprinted: New York: Bantam Books, 1970.

4. Editions with Introductions

The Big Knockover: Selected Stories and Short Novels of Dashiell Hammett. New York: Random House, 1966. Reprinted: New York: Vintage, 1972.

The Selected Letters of Anton Chekhov. New York: Farrar, Straus, and Cudahy, 1955. Reprinted: New York: McGraw-Hill, 1965.

5. Uncollected Articles

"An Aristocrat Who Got Her Education in a Nazi Jail." *New York Star,* November 9, 1948.

"Author Jabs the Critic." *New York Times,* December 15, 1946.

"Back of Those Foxes." *New York Times,* February 26, 1939.

"The Baggage of a Political Exile." *New York Times,* August 23, 1969. [op-ed page]

"Dashiell Hammett: A Memoir." *New York Review of Books,* November 25, 1965, reprinted *The Big Knockover,* and with additions in *An Unfinished Woman,* and in Robert Lyons, ed., *Autobiography: A Reader For Writers.* New York: Oxford University Press, 1977.

"Day in Spain." *New Republic,* April 13, 1938. Reprinted in Curt Reis, ed., *They Were There.* New York: G. P. Putnam's Sons, 1944.

"*H. G. Wells and Rebecca West.*" *New York Times Book Review,* October 13, 1974.

"Home to German-Americans Is Place Called Germany." *New York Star,* November 4, 1948.

"I Call Her Mama Now." *American Spectator,* September, 1933. [signed Lillian Hellman Kober]

"I Meet the Front-Line Russians." *Collier's,* March 31, 1945.

"Interlude in Budapest." *Holiday,* November, 1967.

"Introduction" to Lev Kopelev's *To Be Preserved Forever.* Translated and edited Anthony Austin. Philadelphia and New York: J. B. Lippincott, 1977.

"The Judas Goats." *The Screen Writer,* December, 1947.

"The Land That Holds the Legend of Our Lives." *Ladies' Home Journal,* April, 1964.

"Lillian Hellman Asks a Little Respect for Her Agony: An Eminent Playwright Hallucinates After a Fall Brought On by a Current Dramatic Hit." *Show*, May, 1964.

"The Little Men in Philadelphia." *PM*, June 25, 1940.

"The Little War," in Whitney Burnett, ed., *This Is My Best*. Garden City, N.Y.: Halcyon House, 1944.

"Martinique." *Travel and Leisure*, January, 1974.

"On Jumping into Life." *Mademoiselle*, August, 1975.

"Perberty in Los Angeles." *American Spectator*, January, 1934. [signed Lillian Hellman Kober]

"Plain Speaking with Mrs. Carter." *Rolling Stone*, November 18, 1976. [Report of an interview]

"A Scene from an Unfinished Play." *New Republic*, November 30, 1974.

"Scotch on the Rocks." *New York Review of Books*, October 17, 1963.

"Slavs Warm, But Hard to Understand." *New York Star*, November 7, 1948.

"Sophronia's Grandson Goes to Washington." *Ladies' Home Journal*, December, 1963.

"Stopover at Paris Brings Memories of Spanish War." *New York Star*, November 10, 1948.

"The Time of the 'Foxes.'" *New York Times*, October 22, 1967.

"Tito's 'Personal' Regime Isn't Socialism, Czechs Say." *New York Star*, November 5, 1948.

"Tito, Sure of Strength, Foresees No War." *New York Star*, November 8, 1948.

6. Unpublished Works

"The Beautiful City of Edinburgh." MS., Lillian Hellman Collection, University of Texas, Austin.

"The Blessing." Film script, adaptation of novel by Nancy Mitford. Lillian Hellman Collection, University of Texas, Austin.

"Dear Queen." Play in collaboration with Louis Kronenberger. Copyright December 30, 1932.

"Richard Harding Davis, 1938." MS., Kriendler Collection, Rutgers University, New Brunswick, N.J.

SECONDARY SOURCES

ADLER, JACOB H. *Lillian Hellman*. Austin, Texas: Steck-Vaughn, 1969. Concise, well-written discussion giving standard view of Hellman's plays.

_____. "Miss Hellman's Two Sisters." *Educational Theatre Journal* 15 (May 1963), 112-17. Comparison of *Toys in the Attic* and *The Three Sisters*.

_____. "The Rose and the Fox: Notes on the Southern Drama. In Louis D. Rubin, Jr. and Robert D. Jacobs, eds. *South: Modern Literature in Its Cultural Setting*. Garden City, N.Y.: Doubleday, 1961. Comparison of Hellman and Tennessee Williams.

ADLER, RENATA. "The Guest Word." *New York Times Book Review*, July 9, 1972, p. 39. Novelist and reviewer Adler replies to review of *The Collected Plays* by a friend of John Simon's, commenting that the reviewer "serenely trashed" the entire history of the theater.

ARMATO, PHILIP M. " 'Good and Evil' in Lillian Hellman's *The Children's Hour*." *Educational Theatre Journal* 25 (1973), 443–47. Points out parallel victims-victimizers structure: teachers are first victimizers, then victims.

BANKHEAD, TALLULAH. *Tallulah*. New York: Harper & Brothers, 1952. Contains Miss Bankhead's account of her success in *The Little Foxes* and her running feud with Hellman.

BUCKLEY, WILLIAM, F., JR. "*Scoundrel Time* & Who Is the Ugliest of Them All?" *National Review* 24 (January 21, 1977), 101–06. The fastest tongue on the Right flicks Hellman with a personal attack, keynoted by the *NR* cover, a reproduction of the Hellman Blackglama fur advertisement on which is superimposed in large type "& Who Is the Ugliest of Them All?" Buckley calls *Scoundrel Time* "tasteless, guileful, self-enraptured." "If one feels that paperwork, the formal exchange of vows, is essential to a sacramentally complete union, then perhaps Lillian Hellman was not married to the Communist movement any more than she was married to Dashiell Hammett." "She is elderly, but there is time yet, time to recognize that she should be ashamed of this awful book."

CLARK, BARRETT H. "Lillian Hellman." *College English* 6 (December, 1944), 127–33. Discussion of plays up to and with particular emphasis on *The Searching Wind*.

CLURMAN, HAROLD. "Lillian Hellman's Garden." *New Republic*, March 26, 1951, pp. 21–22. Review of *The Autumn Garden* by the director of the play.

COLLINGE, PATRICIA. "Another Part of the Hubbards." *New Yorker*, March 15, 1947, pp. 29–30. Amusing parody by actress who created the role of Birdie in *The Little Foxes*.

"Communist Infiltration of the Hollywood Motion-Picture Industry—Part 8." *Hearings Before the Committee on Un-American Activities, House of Representatives, Eighty-Second Congress, Second Session, May 21, 1952*. Washington, D.C.: United States Government Printing Office, 1952, pp. 3541–3549. Hellman's testimony.

DOUDNA, CHRISTINE. "A Still Unfinished Woman: A Conversation with

Lillian Hellman." *Rolling Stone*, February 24, 1977, pp. 52–57. Interview in which Hellman discusses feminist movement, movie *Julia*, growing old.

DOWNER, ALAN S. *Fifty Years of American Drama: 1900–1950*. New York: Henry Regnery, 1951. General discussion of Hellman's plays.

DRUTMAN, IRVING. "Hellman: A Stranger in the Theater." *New York Times*, February 27, 1966, pp. 1, 5. Interview about Hellman's disenchantment with the theater.

DUSENBURY, WINIFRED L. *The Theme of Loneliness in Modern American Drama*. Gainesville: University of Florida Press, 1960, pp. 134–49. The isolating effects of the particular socioeconomic conditions of the South as shown in Southern drama.

EATMAN, JAMES. "The Image of American Destiny: *The Little Foxes.*" *Players*, December-January, 1973, pp. 70–73. Socioeconomic interpretation of the play.

FALK, DORIS V. *Lillian Hellman*. New York: Frederick Ungar, 1978. Advertised as a biography drawn from Hellman's works, the book relies on the usual reference sources and interviews and on Hellman's memoirs. Plot summaries of the plays are followed by brief discussion. Falk describes Hellman's characters as despoilers or bystanders. The book also contains discussions of "theatricalism" and realism, the Depression, and World War II.

FELHEIM, MARVIN. "*The Autumn Garden*: Mechanics and Dialectics." *Modern Drama* 3 (September, 1960), 191–95. Compares Hellman and Chekhov.

FLEISCHMAN, EARL. "*The Searching Wind* in the Making." *Quarterly Journal of Speech* 3 (February, 1945), 22–28. Blames Shumlin's direction for play's difficulties.

GARDNER, FRED. *An Interview with Lillian Hellman*. New York: Jeffrey Norton, 1977. Cassette. Recorded in 1969 before an audience.

GOLD, ARTHUR, and FIZDALE, ROBERT. "Lillian Hellman's Creole Cooking: Recipes from an American Woman Playwright." *Vogue*, June, 1974, pp. 98, 150–51. In addition to recipes, Hellman tells anecdotes.

GOULD, JEAN. *Modern American Playwrights*. New York: Dodd, Mead, 1966. The chapter on Hellman leans heavily on the *Paris Review* interview and the Harriman profile.

HARRIMAN, MARGARET CASE. "Miss Lily of New Orleans: Lillian Hellman." In *Take Them Up Tenderly*. New York: Alfred A. Knopf, 1944, pp. 94–109. Often-quoted *New Yorker* profile (November 8, 1941) by the daughter of Frank Case, manager of the Algonquin Hotel.

HEILMAN, ROBERT. *The Iceman, the Arsonist and the Troubled Agent*. Seattle: University of Washington, 1973. Discusses *The Little Foxes* in section "Dramas of Money."

HERSEY, JOHN. "Lillian Hellman." *New Republic*, September 18, 1976, pp. 25–27. Text of the novelist's remarks on presentation of MacDowell Prize to Hellman.

HOOK, SIDNEY. "Lillian Hellman's Scoundrel Time." *Encounter* 48 (February, 1977), 82–91. "Miss Hellman may or may not have been a member of the Communist Party but until Stalin died she was not only a convinced Communist but a Stalinist; and for all her posturing . . . she may still be a Communist." She "loyally cooperated with members of the Communist Party in all sorts of political and cultural enterprises for almost forty years. . . ."

ISAACS, EDITH J. R. "Lillian Hellman: A Playwright on the March." *Theatre Arts*, January, 1944, pp. 19–24. Appraisal of early plays.

KAZIN, ALFRED. "The Legend of Lillian Hellman." *Esquire*, August, 1977, pp. 28, 30, 34. "The many adoring reviews of *Scoundrel Time* . . . were ignorant and simpleminded." "*Scoundrel Time* is historically a fraud, artistically a put-up job and emotionally packed with meanness."

KING, KIMBALL. *The Works of Lillian Hellman.* Deland, Florida: Everett-Edwards, 1976. Cassette. Extremely Freudian interpretation of Hellman's work. Hellman sublimates aggression, attacks audience through her work.

KNELMAN, MARTIN. "Starring . . . the Writer." *Atlantic*, November 19, 1977, pp. 96–98. Review of *Julia*, mostly devoted to discussion of Hellman, who "has become an icon of survival with honor. It is this emergence of the writer as star personality that the movie celebrates."

KNEPLER, HENRY. "Translation and Adaptation in the Contemporary Drama." *Modern Drama* 4 (May, 1961), 31–41. Compares Christopher Fry's translation and Hellman's adaptation of *The Lark* and finds Hellman's version more successful.

LAUFE, ABE. *Anatomy of a Hit: Long-Run Plays on Broadway from 1900 to the Present Day.* New York. Hawthorn, 1966. Discusses *The Children's Hour* and *Toys in the Attic.*

LEWIS, ALLAN. *American Plays and Playwrights of the Contemporary Theatre.* New York: Crown, 1965. General discussion of Hellman's plays.

LEWIS, EMORY. *Stages: The Fifty-Year Childhood of the American Theatre.* Englewood Cliffs, N.J.: Prentice-Hall, 1969. Blames failure of *My Mother, My Father and Me* on direction, production. Quotes Edmund Wilson and others in support.

"Lillian Hellman Looks at Her Own Reflection." In Otis L. Guernsey, Jr., ed. *Playwrights, Lyricists, Composers on Theater.* New York: Dodd, Mead, 1974. Interview in question-answer format at Dramatists Guild Meeting.

MANEY, RICHARD. *Fanfare: The Confessions of a Press Agent.* New York: Harper & Brothers, 1957. Show business reminiscences by publicist for most Hellman plays.

MARJA, FERN. "A Clearing in the Forest." *New York Post*, March 6, 1960. Interview about *Toys in the Attic.*

MEEHAN, THOMAS. "Miss Hellman, What's Wrong with Broadway?" In

Robert Corrigan, ed., *The Modern Theatre*. New York:Macmillan, 1964, pp. 1108–12. Report of interview in question-answer format, reprinted from *Esquire* (December, 1962). Hellman talks about other writers and the emphasis on love and loneliness in modern drama.

MOODY, RICHARD. *Lillian Hellman: Playwright*. New York: Bobbs-Merrill, 1972. This first book-length study contains no original criticism.

NATHAN, GEORGE JEAN. *The Entertainment of a Nation*. New York: Knopf, 1942, pp. 34–40. *Watch on the Rhine* proves that Hellman is the best woman playwright and that the best women writers aren't as good as the best men.

PHILLIPS, JOHN, and HOLLANDER, ANNE. "The Art of the Theater: Lillian Hellman, An Interview." *Paris Review* 33 (Winter-Spring, 1965), 64–95. (Reprinted in George Plimpton, ed., *Writers at Work*. Third Series. New York: Viking, 1968.) The only lengthy interview before the 1970s.

ROUGHEAD, WILLIAM. *Bad Companions*. New York: Duffield and Green, 1931. The essay, "Closed Doors; or, The Great Drumsheugh Case" in this book gave Hellman the idea for *The Children's Hour*.

SHENKER, ISRAEL. *Words and Their Masters*. New York: Doubleday, 1974, pp. 279–81. Contains an interview in which Hellman talks about the student generation.

SIEVERS, W. DAVID. *Freud on Broadway: A History of Psychoanalysis and the American Drama*. New York: Hermitage, 1955, pp. 279–89. Freudian interpretation of Hellman's plays.

SIMON, JOHN. "Pentimental Journey." *Hudson Review* 25 (Winter, 1973–74), 743–52. Ostensibly a review of *Pentimento*, in which Simon complains that Hellman paid a friend of his too little for a translation and that because of difficulties over this matter and others Simon's advisor, who was a friend of Hellman's, almost kept him from graduating.

SPACKS, PATRICIA MEYER. "Free Women." *Hudson Review* 23 (Winter, 1971–72), 559–73. An earlier version of a part of Spacks' *The Female Imagination* (New York: Knopf, 1975).

STERN, RICHARD. "Lillian Hellman on Her Plays." *Contact* 3,i (1959), 113–19. Selection from taped interview in Modern Poetry Collection, University of Chicago.

STILLMAN, DEANNE. "Pimento: Lillian Hellman Reaches into the Pickle Jar of Her Past." In Deanne Stillman and Anne Beatts, eds., *Titters*. New York: Collier, 1976, pp. 56–60. Parody of *Pentimento* in collection of humorous pieces by women.

STYRON, WILLIAM. *Double Exposure*, ed. Roddy McDowell. New York: Delacourte, 1966, pp. 190–93. Affectionate word portrait of Hellman to accompany McDowell photograph.

Sweetest Smelling Baby in New Orleans. Los Angeles: Pacifica Tape Library, 1975. Cassette. Interview, together with excerpts from Hellman plays, films, memoirs.

TRIESCH, MANFRED. *Explicator* 24 (October, 1965), Item 20. Argues that Hellman took title *Another Part of the Forest* from *Titus Andronicus*.

WALCUTT, CHARLES CHILD. *Man's Changing Mask: Modes of Characterization in Fiction*. Minneapolis: University of Minnesota Press, 1966. Discusses characterization of Carrie in *Toys in the Attic*.

Bibliographies

CURLEY, DOROTHY NYREN; KRAMER, MAURICE; and KRAMER, ELAINE FIALKA. *A Library of Literary Criticism: Modern American Literature*. New York: Frederick Ungar, 1969, II, 61–65. Contains selected excerpts from reviews and critical articles.

The New York Times Directory of the Theatre. New York, 1973. Contains title and personal name indexes to all reviews in the *Times* from 1920 to 1970.

SALEM, JAMES M. *A Guide to Critical Reviews. Part I: American Drama, 1909–1969*. Metuchen, N.J.: Scarecrow Press, 1973, pp. 200–206. Lists magazine and nonacademic journal entries for each Hellman play.

TRIESCH, MANFRED. *The Lillian Hellman Collection at the University of Texas*. Austin: The University of Texas, 1966. Bibliographic description of the collection. (Contains errors)

——————. "Lillian Hellman, A Selective Bibliography." *American Book Collector* 14 (June, 1964), 57. (Also contains errors)

VINSON, JAMES. *Contemporary Dramatists*. New York: St. Martin's Press, 1977, pp. 372–74. Biographical paragraph, list of Hellman plays, reprint of Harold Clurman's introduction to Moody's book.

Index

812.52
H477

109 330